D0830998

TWO PLAYS OF SHERIDAN

THE RIVALS AND THE SCHOOL FOR SCANDAL

Two Plays of Sheridan

THE RIVALS *and*
THE SCHOOL FOR SCANDAL

Edited by
GUY BOAS

LONDON
EDWARD ARNOLD (PUBLISHERS) LTD.

This is a revised and reset version
of the original edition by Guy Boas

PRINTED IN GREAT BRITAIN IN THE CITY OF OXFORD
AT THE ALDEN PRESS

CONTENTS

ACKNOWLEDGMENTS

Our thanks for permission to reproduce the photographs on the cover are due to John Vickers Studio and to Houston Rogers, Esq.

The Life of Sheridan

Richard Brinsley Sheridan was born in Dublin in 1751, and at the age of seven was sent to a schoolmaster, Samuel Whyte, with the recommendation from his mother that he was 'an impenetrable dunce'. At eleven Sheridan was sent to Harrow, where according to Dr. Parr, the Headmaster, 'his answers to any common question were prompt and acute'. Somehow or other he gained the admiration of all his schoolfellows; he also kept an extensive apple-loft which he obliged the junior boys to furnish.

While he was at Harrow, Sheridan's mother died, and soon afterwards his father settled at Bath. Here Sheridan became acquainted with a celebrated singer, Miss Linley, 'The Maid of Bath'. Miss Linley had already been admired by a Mr. Long, an old gentleman of considerable wealth. Informed by the lady that she could never love him, Mr. Long not only took upon himself the whole blame for their engagement being broken off, but forestalled an action for breach of promise threatened by Mr. Linley, the lady's father, by settling upon her the sum of £3000. Miss Linley was now pestered with the attentions of a Captain Matthews, who was already married. To save her from this annoyance, Sheridan escorted Miss Linley to a nunnery in France. Captain Matthews inserted in the *Bath Chronicle* insinuations with regard to the disappearance of the young couple, whereupon Sheridan returned promptly from France and fought a duel with Matthews in Hyde Park. Rushing in prematurely on Matthews's guard, Sheridan extracted an apology — subsequently inserted in the *Bath Chronicle* — at the point of the sword. Matthews retired disgruntled to his estate in Wales, where an Irish friend incited him to a second encounter with Sheridan to retrieve his honour. The night before the second duel, which was fought at Bath, Sheridan invited Matthews to supper with him. Sheridan drank deep till the hour of appointment, and then proceeded to totter down Milsom Street. Coming upon Matthews's chaise, which was waiting for its owner, he reeled into it with his seconds, and ordered the driver to take them to the ground, leaving Matthews to follow in a borrowed vehicle. During the duel, which was as violent as it was unskilful, Matthews disarmed Sheridan and directed him to beg for his life. 'No, by God, I won't,' said Sheridan. The seconds intervened. Matthews disappeared to London, and Sheridan was driven back to Bath in a chaise. The matter was reported to Miss Linley, who electrified the nunnery by exclaiming 'My husband! My husband!', whereupon it was revealed that during their expedition she and Sheridan had secretly undergone the marriage ceremony.

The marriage having been made public, Sheridan, who had no income, purchased a London house in Portman Square out of the £3000 bestowed upon his wife by Mr. Long, furnished it lavishly, and proceeded to entertain fashionable society with all the extravagance and fascination of a Charles Surface, and with no more resources. Many stories are told of angry creditors calling upon Sheridan, who would welcome them in his drawing-room, immaculately clad, beg them to share a bottle of the best wine with him, charm them by the wit of his conversation, and send them away exchanging many mutual compliments and almost oblivious of their mission. Servants would starve in his service rather than leave him, and we have descriptions of Sheridan being driven about in a fine coach, for which he had not paid, by a devoted coachman who had received no wages.

Sheridan would not allow his wife to labour for him by continuing any longer as a singer, but resolved to support her by his successful pen. In the January of 1775 his first comedy, *The Rivals*, was produced at Covent Garden

In the same year as *The Rivals* Sheridan's farce, *St. Patrick's Day, or The Scheming Lieutenant*, was produced. In November of the same year, in conjunction with Linley, his father-in-law, who superintended the music, Sheridan produced the comic opera, *The Duenna*, which ran for seventy-five nights at Covent Garden.

In 1776 Sheridan, with the help of his father-in-law and another friend, purchased Garrick's share in Drury Lane, and a few years later bought the complete ownership of the theatre. At Drury Lane in February 1777 he produced *A Trip to Scarborough*, a bowdlerized adaptation which he had made of Vanbrugh's *Relapse*, but this proved a failure. In May 1777, after some conflict with the Lord Chamberlain, he produced *The School for Scandal*, which was enthusiastically received and brought considerable prosperity to Drury Lane. *The Critic* was produced in 1779, and Sheridan's last play, *Pizarro*, a tragedy, in 1799.

In 1780 Sheridan determined to enter politics and was elected to Parliament as member for Stafford. He entertained the voting population of Stafford so lavishly before his election that he had to devote his first speech in Parliament to defending himself against the charge of bribery. He joined the Opposition under Burke and Fox, opposed the American War, and when Lord North's Ministry resigned in 1782 became Under-Secretary for Foreign Affairs under Rockingham, and later Secretary to the Treasury under the coalition Ministry of 1783.

Sheridan found the opportunity of making a considerable parliamentary reputation at the Impeachment of Warren Hastings. When the trial took place in Westminster Hall, Burke, Fox and Sheridan were the accusers. Sheridan delivered three great speeches, in which he exposed the manner in which Hastings had forcibly seized the treasure of the begums, or princesses, of Oude, to provide funds for fighting the French in India. When the question of the impeachment was first raised in the House of Commons, Sheridan spoke for five hours and the effect of his oratory was so overwhelming that it was decided to adjourn the voting of the House till the next day, when it might be in more dispassionate temper.

Although Sheridan sat in Parliament for thirty-two years, except for an occasional oratorical *tour de force*, such as his powerful speech supporting the suppression of the mutiny at the Nore, his natural indolence prevented him from sustaining his reputation, and his achievement fell short of his ability. Although a close companion of the Prince of Wales, who in 1811 became Prince Regent, Sheridan's parliamentary work was never crowned by any substantial office, and in 1812, when he was defeated at the polls at Westminster, his political career came to an end.

The close of Sheridan's life was one of gloom and poverty. In 1792 his first wife had died, and three years later he married a Miss Ogle, daughter of the Dean of Winchester, who survived him. On an evening in February 1809 Drury Lane Theatre, which represented Sheridan's substance, was burnt to the ground, and he was ruined. Sheridan was in the House of Commons when the news of the disaster was brought. The Speaker proposed an adjournment, but Sheridan protested with complete nonchalance against such an interruption. Having eventually arrived at the scene of the catastrophe, he sat down with a friend to watch the conflagration from a neighbouring coffee-house, and ordered a bottle of port, remarking that it was 'hard if a man could not drink a glass of wine by his own fireside'.

So long as he was a Member of Parliament Sheridan had been safe against being arrested for debt, but now that this protection no longer covered him his creditors became importunate, and bailiffs took possession of his house when he was lying mortally sick of an internal disorder which had for some time threatened him. A sheriff's officer was on the point of arresting the dying man in his bed and carrying him off to prison in his blankets, had not Sheridan's doctor warned him of the responsibility which he would incur if his prisoner should die on the journey.

An article in the *Morning Post* roused the public to a realization of the situation, and friends hurried to the bedside. Their help was unpunctual and fruitless, and, after fits of shivering, on July 7th, 1816, Sheridan fell into a condition of complete exhaustion and died.

Shortly before he became unconscious on his death-bed, Sheridan whispered, 'Tell Lady Bessborough that my eyes will look up to the coffin-lid as brightly as ever.'

In spite of the painful circumstances of his death, the eyes of Sheridan still sparkle through his brilliant comedies and the numberless gay anecdotes which cluster about his name, and shine upon his posterity as brightly as he promised.

The Rivals

INTRODUCTION

Sheridan is an exception to the rule that, while young men are as likely to write first-class poetry as old men, they are less likely to write first-class prose.

Sheridan had written all his comedies by the time he was twenty-eight, and he wrote *The Rivals*, his first, when he was only twenty-three. The play was produced at Covent Garden on January 17th, 1775. It was not favourably received, and was therefore withdrawn to be reduced in length, and a more competent actor was found to take the part of Sir Lucius O'Trigger. Thus renovated it was produced again on January 28th, and found the favour which it has never lost.

The Rivals, as well as making Sheridan's name as a playwright, marked a stage in the history of English drama. In a Prologue, which the author added to be spoken on the tenth night, after the play had succeeded, Sheridan attacks the sentimental comedy of the day in which insipidity had taken the place of the licence of Restoration comedy, and dialogue had become a string of sentiments.

The English drama in the age preceding Sheridan was in a low condition. Between the close of the Restoration period and the production of Goldsmith's *She Stoops to Conquer* in 1773, hardly a play is known to any but dramatic students.

In 1698 Jeremy Collier had published his *Short View of the Profaneness and Immorality of the English Stage*, which had made a deep impression. In Queen Anne's reign societies were formed for the reformation of manners. In 1717 an Act was passed confining the presentation of drama in London to Covent Garden and Drury Lane and requiring all plays to be submitted to a Government censor. The puritanical revival begun by John Wesley in 1739 further purged public taste, and, as no first-rate dramatist was forthcoming, English comedy became dull and insipid. Goldsmith, in dedicating *She Stoops to Conquer* to Dr. Johnson, writes: 'The undertaking a comedy not merely sentimental was very dangerous.'

Encouraged no doubt by the success of Goldsmith's venture, Sheridan in *The Rivals* is clearly out to amuse rather than to improve his audience. Only the scenes between Faulkland and Julia remain somewhat of an enigma. In these scenes, in which the lovers asphyxiate one another with clouds of sentiment, Sheridan seems to be inflicting on the audience the very commodity which he is undertaking to supersede. It is commonly held that, while Sheridan is striking out the new style, he cannot, in his first play, throw over tradition altogether; that he cannot risk sending away the sentiment-loving portion of his audience completely empty: that in these scenes he caters for them, so that the play is a link between the past and the future.

It is a common amusement among those who have never themselves benefited humanity by a masterpiece to try to detract from the achievement of Sheridan by pointing out how unoriginal he was. Dogberry, they triumphantly remind us, mispronounced words before Mrs. Malaprop; so did Mrs. Tryfort, a citizen's wife in *A Journey to Bath*, an unpublished novel by Sheridan's mother, and Mrs. Slipslop in *Joseph Andrews*: Acres resembles Sir Andrew Aguecheek, and David might have belonged to the domestic staff of Goldsmith's Mr. Hardcastle. To all of which it may be answered that this is perfectly true, and it is also always possible that one of the critics might himself at the age of twenty-three have produced a comedy as amusing, as well constructed, as fresh, as vital, and as exciting as *The Rivals*, but that he did not do so and that Sheridan did, and that in any case, to mingle the language of Mrs. Malaprop and Dogberry, 'caparisons are odorous'.

THE CAST

SIR ANTHONY ABSOLUTE
CAPTAIN ABSOLUTE, *his son*
FAULKLAND, *engaged to Julia*
ACRES, *a boorish young man, neighbour to Sir Anthony*
SIR LUCIUS O'TRIGGER, *a spendthrift Irish baronet*
FAG, *servant to Captain Absolute*
DAVID, *servant to Acres*
THOMAS, *servant to Sir Anthony*
MRS. MALAPROP
LYDIA LANGUISH, *neice to Mrs. Malaprop*
JULIA MELVILLE, *cousin to Lydia*
LUCY, *maid to Lydia*
MAID, BOY, SERVANTS, ETC.

Scene: Fashionable Bath in 1775

ACT I

Scene I. *A Street in Bath*

Enter THOMAS; *he crosses the stage;* FAG *follows, looking after him*

FAG. What! Thomas! sure 'tis he? — What! Thomas! Thomas!

THOMAS. Hey! — Odd's life! Mr. Fag! — give us your hand, my old fellow-servant.

FAG. Excuse my glove, Thomas: — I'm devilish glad to see you, my lad. Why, my prince of charioteers, you look as hearty — but who the deuce thought of seeing you in Bath?

THOMAS. Sure, master, Madam Julia, Harry, Mrs. Kate, and the postillion, be all come. 10

FAG. Indeed!

THOMAS. Ay, master thought another fit of the gout was coming to make him a visit; — so he'd a mind to gi't the slip, and whip! we were all off at an hour's warning.

FAG. Ay, ay, hasty in everything, or it would not be Sir Anthony Absolute!

THOMAS. But tell us, Mr. Fag, how does young master? Odd! Sir Anthony will stare to see the Captain here!

FAG. I do not serve Captain Absolute now.

THOMAS. Why sure! 20

FAG. At present I am employed by Ensign Beverley.

---

l.3 Odd's life: *corruption of 'God's life'.*
l.10 the postillion: *the coachman of an eighteenth-century post-chaise did not drive all the horses but left the leading pair to a postillion who rode the near-side leader.*
l.21 Ensign: *present-day Second Lieutenant.*

THOMAS. I doubt, Mr. Fag, you ha'n't changed for the better.

FAG. I have not changed, Thomas.

THOMAS. No! Why, didn't you say you had left young master?

FAG. No. — Well, honest Thomas, I must puzzle you no farther: — briefly then — Captain Absolute and Ensign Beverley are one and the same person.

30 THOMAS. The devil they are!

FAG. So it is indeed, Thomas; and the ensign half of my master being on guard at present — the captain has nothing to do with me.

THOMAS. So, so! — What, this is some freak, I warrant! — Do tell us, Mr. Fag, the meaning o't — you know I ha' trusted you.

FAG. You'll be secret, Thomas?

THOMAS. As a coach-horse.

FAG. Why then the cause of all this is — Love, — Love,
40 Thomas, who, (as you may get read to you,) has been a masquerader ever since the days of Jupiter.

THOMAS. Ay, ay; — I guessed there was a lady in the case: — but pray, why does you master pass only for ensign? — Now if he had shammed general indeed ——

FAG. Ah! Thomas, there lies the mystery o' the matter. Hark'ee, Thomas, my master is in love with a lady of a very singular taste: a lady who likes him better as a half pay ensign than if she knew he was son and heir to Sir Anthony Absolute, a baronet of three thousand a year.

50 THOMAS. That is an odd taste indeed! — But has she got the stuff, Mr. Fag? Is she rich, hey?

---

ll.39-41 Love ... a masquerader ever since the days of Jupiter: *Jupiter, according to legend, assumed the form of a bull to court the Phœnician princess Europa.*

FAG. Rich! — Why, I believe she owns half the stocks! Zounds! Thomas, she could pay the national debt as easily as I could my washer-woman! She has a lapdog that eats out of gold, — she feeds her parrot with small pearls, — and all her thread-papers are made of bank-notes.

THOMAS. Bravo, faith! — Odd! I warrant she has a set of thousands at least: — but does she draw kindly with the captain?

FAG. As fond as pigeons.   60

THOMAS. May one hear her name?

FAG. Miss Lydia Languish. — But there is an old tough aunt in the way; though, by the by, she has never seen my master — for we got acquainted with miss while on a visit in Gloucestershire.

THOMAS. Well — I wish they were once harnessed together in matrimony. — But pray, Mr. Fag, what kind of a place is this Bath? — I ha' heard a deal of it — here's a mort o' merry-making, hey?

FAG. Pretty well, Thomas, pretty well — 'tis a good lounge; 70 in the morning we go to the Pump Room (though neither my master nor I drink the waters); after breakfast we saunter on the parades, or play a game at billiards; at night we dance; but I'm tired of the place: their regular hours stupify me — not a fiddle nor a card after eleven! — However, Mr. Faulkland's gentleman and I keep it up a little in private parties; — I'll introduce you there, Thomas — you'll like him much.

THOMAS. Sure I know Mr. Du-Peigne — you know his master is to marry Madam Julia.   80

---

l.56 thread-papers: *strips of paper for wrapping up skeins of thread.*
ll.57-8 set of thousands: *a set of horses worth £1000.*
l.71 Pump Room: *then, as now, a leading social centre in Bath.*
l.72 drink the waters: *take the medicinal water for which Bath was, and is, famous.*

FAG. I had forgot. — But, Thomas, you must polish a little — indeed you must. — Here now — this wig! — What the devil do you do with a wig, Thomas? — None of the London whips of any degree of *ton* wear wigs now.

THOMAS. More's the pity! more's the pity, I say. — Odd's life! when I heard how the lawyers and doctors had took to their own hair, I thought how 'twould go next: — odd rabbit it! when the fashion had got foot on the bar, I guessed 'twould mount to the box! — but 'tis all out of
90 character, believe me, Mr. Fag: and look'ee, I'll never gi' up mine — the lawyers and doctors may do as they will.

FAG. Well, Thomas, we'll not quarrel about that.

THOMAS. Why, bless you, the gentlemen of the professions ben't all of a mind — for in our village now, thoff Jack Gauge, the exciseman, has ta'en to his carrots, there's little Dick the farrier swears he'll never forsake his bob, though all the college should appear with their own heads!

FAG. Indeed! well said, Dick! — But hold — mark! mark!
100 Thomas.

THOMAS. Zooks! 'tis the captain. — Is that the lady with him?

FAG. No, no, that is Madam Lucy, my master's mistress's maid. They lodge at that house — but I must after him to tell him the news.

---

ll.82-3 What the devil do you do with a wig, Thomas?: *by* 1775 *wigs were beginning to become unfashionable.*
l.84 whip: *the driver of a coach*; ton: *fashion.*
ll.87-8 odd rabbit it: *Confound it!*
l.88 the bar: *by means of which one stepped up on to the box-seat of a coach.*
l.94 thoff: *though.*
l.95 exciseman: *a Customs official*; his carrots: *his own carrot-coloured hair.*
ll.96-7 farrier … all the college: *will not forsake his bob wig, though all the college of veterinary surgeons should appear with their own hair (i.e. without wigs).*

THOMAS. Odd! he's giving her money! — Well, Mr. Fag——

FAG. Good-bye, Thomas. I have an appointment in Gyde's Porch this evening at eight; meet me there, and we'll make a little party. [*Exeunt severally.*

SCENE II. *A Dressing-room in Mrs. Malaprop's Lodgings*

LYDIA *sitting on a sofa, with a book in her hand.* LUCY, *as just returned from a message*

LUCY. Indeed, ma'am, I traversed half the town in search of it: I don't believe there's a circulating library in Bath I ha'n't been at.

LYDIA. And could not you get *The Reward of Constancy*?

LUCY. No, indeed, ma'am.

LYDIA. Nor *The Fatal Connection*?

LUCY. No, indeed, ma'am.

LYDIA. Nor *The Mistakes of the Heart*?

LUCY. Ma'am, as ill luck would have it, Mr. Bull said Miss Sukey Saunter had just fetched it away. 10

LYDIA. Heigh-ho! — Did you inquire for *The Delicate Distress*?

LUCY. Or, *The Memoirs of Lady Woodford*? Yes, indeed, ma'am. I asked everywhere for it; and I might have brought it from Mr. Frederick's, but Lady Slattern Lounger, who had just sent it home, had so soiled and dog's-eared it, it wa'n't fit for a Christian to read.

LYDIA. Heigh-ho! — Yes, I always know when Lady Slattern has been before me. She has a most observing thumb; and I believe, cherishes her nails for the conveni- 20 ence of making marginal notes. — Well, child, what have you brought me?

---

ll.107-8 Gyde's Porch: *another fashionable centre in Bath.*
l.4 The Reward of Constancy: *of the various books to which the ladies refer* Peregrine Pickle, Humphrey Clinker, *both by Smollett, and* A Sentimental Journey *by Sterne have achieved lasting fame.*

LUCY. Oh! here, ma'am. — [*Taking books from under her cloak, and from her pockets.*] This is *The Gordian Knot*, — and this *Peregrine Pickle*. Here are *The Tears of Sensibility*, and *Humphrey Clinker*. This is *The Memoirs of a Lady of Quality, written by herself*, and here the second volume of *A Sentimental Journey*.

LYDIA. Heigh-ho! — What are those books by the glass?

30 LUCY. The great one is only *The Whole Duty of Man*, where I press a few blonds, ma'am.

LYDIA. Very well — give me the sal volatile.

LUCY. Is it in a blue cover, ma'am?

LYDIA. My smelling-bottle, you simpleton!

LUCY. Oh, the drops! — here, ma'am.

LYDIA. Hold! — here's some one coming — quick, see who it is. — [*Exit* LUCY.] Surely I heard my cousin Julia's voice.

Re-enter LUCY

LUCY. Lud! ma'am, here is Miss Melville.

LYDIA. Is it possible! — [*Exit* LUCY.

Enter JULIA

40 LYDIA. My dearest Julia, how delighted am I! — [*Embrace.*] How unexpected was this happiness!

JULIA. True, Lydia — and our pleasure is the greater. — But what has been the matter? — you were denied to me at first!

LYDIA. Ah, Julia, I have a thousand things to tell you! — But first inform me what has conjured you to Bath? — Is Sir Anthony here?

JULIA. He is — we are arrived within this hour! — and I suppose he will be here to wait on Mrs. Malaprop as soon
50 as he is dressed.

---

l.31 blonds: *silk laces blond in colour.*

LYDIA. Then before we are interrupted, let me impart to you some of my distress! — I know your gentle nature will sympathize with me, though your prudence may condemn me! My letters have informed you of my whole connection with Beverley; but I have lost him, Julia! My aunt has discovered our intercourse by a note she intercepted, and has confined me ever since! Yet, would you believe it? she has absolutely fallen in love with a tall Irish baronet she met one night since we have been here, at Lady Macshuffle's rout. 60

JULIA. You jest, Lydia!

LYDIA. No, upon my word. — She really carries on a kind of correspondence with him, under a feigned name though, till she chooses to be known to him; — but it is a Delia or a Celia, I assure you.

JULIA. Then, surely, she is now more indulgent to her neice.

LYDIA. Quite the contrary. Since she has discovered her own frailty, she is become more suspicious of mine. Then I must inform you of another plague! — That odious 70 Acres is to be in Bath to-day; so that I protest I shall be teased out of all spirits!

JULIA. Come, come, Lydia, hope for the best — Sir Anthony shall use his interest with Mrs. Malaprop.

LYDIA. But you have not heard the worst. Unfortunately I had quarrelled with my poor Beverley, just before my aunt made the discovery, and I have not seen him since, to make it up.

JULIA. What was his offence?

LYDIA. Nothing at all! — But, I don't know how it was, as 80 often as we had been together, we had never had a quarrel, and, somehow, I was afraid he would never give me an opportunity. So, last Thursday, I wrote a letter to myself, to inform myself that Beverley was at that time

---

l.60 rout: *a large, fashionable party.*

paying his addresses to another woman. I signed it *your friend unknown*, showed it to Beverley, charged him with his falsehood, put myself in a violent passion, and vowed I'd never see him more.

JULIA. And you let him depart so, and have not seen him
90 since?

LYDIA. 'Twas the next day my aunt found the matter out. I intended only to have teased him three days and a half, and now I've lost him for ever.

JULIA. If he is as deserving and sincere as you have represented him to me, he will never give you up so. Yet consider, Lydia, you tell me he is but an ensign, and you have thirty thousand pounds.

LYDIA. But you know I lose most of my fortune if I marry without my aunt's consent, till of age; and that is what I
100 have determined to do, ever since I knew the penalty. Nor could I love the man who would wish to wait a day for the alternative.

JULIA. Nay, this is caprice!

LYDIA. What, does Julia tax me with caprice? — I thought her lover Faulkland had inured her to it.

JULIA. I do not love even his faults.

LYDIA. But apropos — you have sent to him, I suppose?

JULIA. Not yet, upon my word — nor has he the least idea of my being in Bath. Sir Anthony's resolution was so
110 sudden, I could not inform him of it.

LYDIA. Well, Julia, you are your own mistress, (though under the protection of Sir Anthony,) yet have you, for this long year, been a slave to the caprice, the whim, the jealousy of this ungrateful Faulkland, who will ever delay assuming the right of a husband, while you suffer him to be equally imperious as a lover.

JULIA. Nay, you are wrong entirely. We were contracted before my father's death. That, and some consequent embarrassments, have delayed what I know to be my Faulkland's most ardent wish. He is too generous to 120 trifle on such a point: — and for his character, you wrong him there too. No, Lydia, he is too proud, too noble to be jealous; if he is captious, 'tis without dissembling; if fretful, without rudeness. Unused to the fopperies of love, he is negligent of the little duties expected from a lover — but being unhackneyed in the passion, his affection is ardent and sincere; and as it engrosses his whole soul, he expects every thought and emotion of his mistress to move in unison with his. Yet, though his pride calls for this full return, his humility makes him undervalue 130 those qualities in him which would entitle him to it; and not feeling why he should be loved to the degree he wishes, he still suspects that he is not loved enough. This temper, I must own, has cost me many unhappy hours; but I have learned to think myself his debtor, for those imperfections which arise from the ardour of his attachment.

LYDIA. Well, I cannot blame you for defending him. But tell me candidly, Julia, had he never saved your life, do you think you should have been attached to him as you 140 are? — Believe me, the rude blast that overset your boat was a prosperous gale of love to him.

JULIA. Gratitude may have strengthened my attachment to Mr. Faulkland, but I loved him before he had preserved me; yet surely that alone were an obligation sufficient.

LYDIA. Obligation! why a water spaniel would have done as much! — Well, I should never think of giving my heart to a man because he could swim.

JULIA. Come, Lydia, you are too inconsiderate.

LYDIA. Nay, I do but jest. — What's here? 150

Re-enter LUCY *in a hurry*

LUCY. O ma'am, here is Sir Anthony Absolute just come home with your aunt.

LYDIA. They'll not come here. — Lucy, do you watch.

[Exit LUCY.

JULIA. Yet I must go. Sir Anthony does not know I am here, and if we meet, he'll detain me, to show me the town. I'll take another opportunity of paying my respects to Mrs. Malaprop, when she shall treat me, as long as she chooses, with her select words so ingeniously misapplied, without being mispronounced.

Re-enter LUCY

160 LUCY. O Lud! ma'am, they are both coming upstairs.

LYDIA. Well, I'll not detain you, coz. — Adieu, my dear Julia, I'm sure you are in haste to send to Faulkland. — There — through my room you'll find another staircase.

JULIA. Adieu! *[Embraces LYDIA and exit.*

LYDIA. Here, my dear Lucy, hide these books. Quick, quick. — Fling *Peregrine Pickle* under the toilet — throw *Roderick Random* into the closet — thrust *Lord Aimworth* under the sofa — cram *Ovid* behind the bolster — there — put *The Man of Feeling* into your pocket — so, so — now
170 lay *Mrs. Chapone* in sight, and leave *Fordyce's Sermons* open on the table.

LUCY. O burn it, ma'am! the hairdresser has torn away as far as *Proper Pride.*

LYDIA. Never mind — open at *Sobriety.* — Fling me *Lord Chesterfield's Letters.* — Now for 'em. *[Exit LUCY.*

Enter MRS. MALAPROP, and SIR ANTHONY ABSOLUTE

---

l.166 toilet: *dressing table.*
l.167 Roderick Random: *another famous novel by Smollett.*
l.168 Ovid: *the Roman poet.*
l.170 Mrs. Chapone: *authoress of* Letters on the Improvement of the Mind; Fordyce: *author of* Sermons to Young Women.
ll.174-5 Lord Chesterfield's Letters: *a famous, highly improving work addressed by his lordship to his son.*

MRS. MALAPROP. There, Sir Anthony, there sits the deliberate simpleton who wants to disgrace her family, and lavish herself on a fellow not worth a shilling.

LYDIA. Madam, I thought you once ——

MRS. MALAPROP. You thought, miss! I don't know any 180 business you have to think at all — thought does not become a young woman. But the point we would request of you is, that you will promise to forget this fellow — to illiterate him, I say, quite from your memory.

LYDIA. Ah, madam! Our memories are independent of our wills. It is not so easy to forget.

MRS. MALAPROP. But I say it is, miss; there is nothing on earth so easy as to forget, if a person chooses to set about it. I'm sure I have as much forgot your poor dear uncle as if he had never existed — and I thought it my duty so to do; 190 and let me tell you, Lydia, these violent memories don't become a young woman.

SIR ANTHONY. Why sure she won't pretend to remember what she's ordered not! — ay, this comes of her reading!

LYDIA. What crime, madam, have I committed, to be treated thus?

MRS. MALAPROP. Now don't attempt to extirpate yourself from the matter; you know I have proof controvertible of it. — But tell me, will you promise to do as you're bid? Will you take a husband of your friends' choosing?   200

LYDIA. Madam, I must tell you plainly, that had I no preference for anyone else, the choice you have made would be my aversion.

MRS. MALAPROP. What business have you, miss, with preference and aversion? They don't become a young woman; and you ought to know, that as both always wear off, 'tis safest in matrimony to begin with a little aversion. I am

---

l.184 illiterate: *this is the first of the famous 'Malapropisms'; many more occur throughout the play. To think of the correct word which Mrs. Malaprop really means is a pleasant exercise.*

sure I hated your poor dear uncle before marriage as if he had been a blackamoor — and yet, miss, you are sensible what a wife I made! — and when it pleased Heaven to release me from him, 'tis unknown what tears I shed! — But suppose we were going to give you another choice, will you promise us to give up this Beverley?

LYDIA. Could I belie my thoughts so far as to give that promise, my actions would certainly as far belie my words.

MRS. MALAPROP. Take yourself to your room. — You are fit company for nothing but your own ill-humours.

LYDIA. Willingly, ma'am — I cannot change for the worse.
[*Exit.*

MRS. MALAPROP. There's a little intricate hussy for you!

SIR ANTHONY. It is not to be wondered at, ma'am, — all this is the natural consequence of teaching girls to read. Had I a thousand daughters, by Heaven! I'd as soon have them taught the black art as their alphabet!

MRS. MALAPROP. Nay, nay, Sir Anthony, you are an absolute misanthropy.

SIR ANTHONY. In my way hither, Mrs. Malaprop, I observed your niece's maid coming forth from a circulating library! — She had a book in each hand — they were half-bound volumes, with marble covers! — From that moment I guessed how full of duty I should see her mistress!

MRS. MALAPROP. Those are vile places, indeed!

SIR ANTHONY. Madam, a circulating library in a town is as an evergreen tree of diabolical knowledge! It blossoms through the year! — and depend on it, Mrs. Malaprop, that they who are so fond of handling the leaves, will long for the fruit at last.

---

l.209 you are sensible: *you know.*
l.224 the black art: *sorcery.*
l.226 misanthropy: *misanthrope, one who hates mankind.*
l.230 marble covers: *covers made to resemble marble.*

MRS. MALAPROP. Fie, fie, Sir Anthony! you surely speak laconically.

SIR ANTHONY. Why, Mrs. Malaprop, in moderation now, what would you have a woman know? 240

MRS. MALAPROP. Observe me, Sir Anthony. I would by no means wish a daughter of mine to be a progeny of learning; I don't think so much learning becomes a young woman: for instance, I would never let her meddle with Greek or Hebrew, or algebra, or simony, or fluxions, or paradoxes, or such inflammatory branches of learning — neither would it be necessary for her to handle any of your mathematical, astronomical, diabolical instruments. — But, Sir Anthony, I would send her, at nine years old, to a boarding-school, in order to learn a little ingenuity 250 and artifice. Then, sir, she should have a supercilious knowledge in accounts; — and as she grew up, I would have her instructed in geometry, that she might know something of the contagious countries; — but above all, Sir Anthony, she should be mistress of orthodoxy, that she might not mis-spell, and mis-pronounce words so shamefully as girls usually do; and likewise that she might reprehend the true meaning of what she is saying. This, Sir Anthony, is what I would have a woman know; — and I don't think there is a superstitious article in it. 260

SIR ANTHONY. Well, well, Mrs. Malaprop, I will dispute the point no further with you; though I must confess, that you are a truly moderate and polite arguer, for almost every third word you say is on my side of the question. But, Mrs. Malaprop, to the more important point in debate — you say you have no objection to my proposal?

MRS. MALAPROP. None, I assure you. I am under no positive engagement with Mr. Acres, and as Lydia is so obstinate against him, perhaps your son may have better 270 success.

---

l.246 simony: *simony is the crime of corruptly selling ecclesiastical benefices and preferments for money. Clearly Mrs. Malaprop does not mean this, but what word she intends is obscure.*

SIR ANTHONY. Well, madam, I will write for the boy directly. He knows not a syllable of this yet, though I have for some time had the proposal in my head. He is at present with his regiment.

MRS. MALAPROP. We have never seen your son, Sir Anthony; but I hope no objection on his side.

SIR ANTHONY. Objection! — let him object if he dare! — No, no, Mrs. Malaprop, Jack knows that the least demur puts me in a frenzy directly. My process was always very simple — in their younger days, 'twas 'Jack, do this;' — if he demurred, I knocked him down — and if he grumbled at that, I always sent him out of the room.

MRS. MALAPROP. Ay, and the properest way, o' my conscience! — nothing is so conciliating to young people as severity. — Well, Sir Anthony, I shall give Mr. Acres his discharge, and prepare Lydia to receive your son's invocations; — and I hope you will represent her to the captain as an object not altogether illegible.

SIR ANTHONY. Madam, I will handle the subject prudently. — Well, I must leave you; and let me beg you, Mrs. Malaprop, to enforce this matter roundly to the girl. — Take my advice — keep a tight hand: if she rejects this proposal, clap her under lock and key; and if you were just to let the servants forget to bring her dinner for three or four days, you can't conceive how she'd come about.
[*Exit.*

MRS. MALAPROP. Well, at any rate I shall be glad to get her from under my intuition. She has somehow discovered my partiality for Sir Lucius O'Trigger — sure, Lucy can't have betrayed me! — No, the girl is such a simpleton, I should have made her confess it. [*Calls.*] — Lucy! — Lucy! Had she been one of your artificial ones, I should never have trusted her.

Re-enter LUCY

LUCY. Did you call, ma'am?

MRS. MALAPROP. Yes, girl. — Did you see Sir Lucius while you was out?

LUCY. No, indeed, ma'am, not a glimpse of him.

MRS. MALAPROP. You are sure, Lucy, that you never mentioned ——

LUCY. O gemini! I'd sooner cut my tongue out.   310

MRS. MALAPROP. Well, don't let your simplicity be imposed on.

LUCY. No, ma'am.

MRS. MALAPROP. So, come to me presently, and I'll give you another letter to Sir Lucius; but mind, Lucy — if ever you betray what you are entrusted with (unless it be other people's secrets to me) you forfeit my malevolence for ever; and your being a simpleton shall be no excuse for your locality.   [*Exit.*

LUCY. Ha! ha! ha! — So, my dear Simplicity, let me give 320 you a little respite. — [*Altering her manner.*] Let girls in my station be as fond as they please of appearing expert and knowing in their trusts; commend me to a mask of silliness, and a pair of sharp eyes for my own interest under it! — Let me see to what account have I turned my simplicity lately. — [*Looks at a paper.*] For *abetting Miss Lydia Languish in a design of running away with an ensign! — in money, sundry times, twelve pound twelve; gowns, five; hats, ruffles, caps, &c. &c., numberless! — From the said ensign, within this last month, six guineas and a half.* — 330 About a quarter's pay! — Item, *from Mrs. Malaprop, for betraying the young people to her* — when I found matters were likely to be discovered — *two guineas, and a black paduasoy.* — Item, *from Mr. Acres, for carrying divers letters* — which I never delivered — *two guineas, and a pair of buckles.* — Item, *from Sir Lucius O'Trigger, three*

---

l.329 ruffles: *strips of lace, or cloth plaited so as to form a trimming.*
l.334 paduasoy: *a rich heavy silk coming originally from Padua.*

crowns, two gold pocket-pieces, and a silver snuff-box! —
Well done, Simplicity! — Yet I was forced to make my
Hibernian believe, that he was corresponding, not with
340 the aunt, but with the niece: for though not over rich, I
found he had too much pride and delicacy to sacrifice the
feelings of a gentleman to the necessities of his fortune.

[*Exit.*

ACT II

Scene I. *Captain Absolute's Lodgings*

captain absolute *and* fag

FAG. Sir, while I was there Sir Anthony came in: I told him,
you had sent me to inquire after his health, and to know
if he was at leisure to see you.

ABSOLUTE. And what did he say, on hearing I was at Bath?

FAG. Sir, in my life I never saw an elderly gentleman more
astonished! He started back two or three paces, rapped
out a dozen interjectural oaths, and asked, what the devil
had brought you here.

ABSOLUTE. Well, sir, and what did you say?

10 FAG. Oh, I lied, sir — I forget the precise lie; but you may
depend on't, he got no truth from me. Yet, with submission, for fear of blunders in future, I should be glad to
fix what has brought us to Bath; in order that we may lie
a little consistently. Sir Anthony's servants were curious,
sir, very curious indeed.

ABSOLUTE. You have said nothing to them?

---

l.337 crowns: *worth 5s.*; pocket-pieces: *coins which cannot be spent
as they are not current, and so kept in the pocket.*
l.339 Hibernian: *an inhabitant of Ireland (Hibernia).*
l.7 interjectural: *thrown in between other words.*

FAG. Oh, not a word, sir, — not a word! Mr. Thomas, indeed, the coachman (whom I take to be the discreetest of whips) ——

ABSOLUTE. 'Sdeath! — you rascal! you have not trusted 20 him!

FAG. Oh, no, sir — no — no — not a syllable, upon my veracity! — He was, indeed, a little inquisitive; but I was sly, sir — devilish sly! My master (said I), honest Thomas (you know, sir, one says honest to one's inferiors), is come to Bath to recruit — Yes, sir, I said to recruit — and whether for men, money, or constitution, you know, sir, is nothing to him, nor anyone else.

ABSOLUTE. Well, recruit will do — let it be so.

FAG. Oh, sir, recruit will do surprisingly — indeed, to give 30 the thing an air, I told Thomas, that your honour had already enlisted five disbanded chairmen, seven minority waiters, and thirteen billiard-markers.

ABSOLUTE. You blockhead, never say more than is necessary.

FAG. I beg pardon, sir — I beg pardon — but, with submission, a lie is nothing unless one supports it. Sir, whenever I draw on my invention for a good current lie, I always forge indorsements as well as the bill.

ABSOLUTE. Well, take care you don't hurt your credit, by offering too much security. — Is Mr. Faulkland re- 40 turned?

FAG. He is above, sir, changing his dress.

ABSOLUTE. Can you tell whether he has been informed of Sir Anthony and Miss Melville's arrival?

---

l.32 chairmen: *either carriers of the sedan-chair or drawers of the invalid bath-chair.*
ll.32-3 minority waiters: *unemployed waiters.*
l.38 indorsements: *writing on the back of a bill guaranteeing payment.*

FAG. I fancy not, sir; he has seen no one since he came in but his gentleman, who was with him at Bristol. — I think, sir, I hear Mr. Faulkland coming down ——

ABSOLUTE. Go, tell him I am here.

50 FAG. Yes, sir. — [*Going.*] I beg pardon, sir, but should Sir Anthony call, you will do me the favour to remember that we are recruiting, if you please.

ABSOLUTE. Well, well.

FAG. And, in tenderness to my character, if your honour could bring in the chairmen and waiters, I should esteem it as an obligation; for though I never scruple a lie to serve my master, yet it hurts one's conscience to be found out.   [*Exit.*

ABSOLUTE. Now for my whimsical friend — if he does not know that his mistress is here, I'll tease him a little before 60 I tell him —

Enter FAULKLAND

Faulkland, you're welcome to Bath again; you are punctual in your return.

FAULKLAND. Yes; I had nothing to detain me, when I had finished the business I went on. Well, what news since I left you? how stand matters between you and Lydia?

ABSOLUTE. Faith, much as they were; I have not seen her since our quarrel; however, I expect to be recalled every hour.

FAULKLAND. Why don't you persuade her to go off with 70 you at once?

ABSOLUTE. What, and lose two-thirds of her fortune? you forget that, my friend. — No, no, I could have brought her to that long ago.

FAULKLAND. Nay then, you trifle too long — if you are sure of her, propose to the aunt in your own character, and write to Sir Anthony for his consent.

ABSOLUTE. Softly, softly; for though I am convinced my little Lydia would elope with me as Ensign Beverley, yet am I by no means certain that she would take me with the impediment of our friends' consent, a regular humdrum 80 wedding, and the reversion of a good fortune on my side: no, no; I must prepare her gradually for the discovery, and make myself necessary to her, before I risk it. — Well, but, Faulkland, you'll dine with us to-day at the hotel?

FAULKLAND. Indeed I cannot; I am not in spirits to be of such a party.

ABSOLUTE. By Heavens! I shall forswear your company. You are the most teasing, captious, incorrigible lover! — Do love like a man.

FAULKLAND. I own I am unfit for company.   90

ABSOLUTE. Am not I a lover; ay, and a romantic one too? Yet do I carry everywhere with me such a confounded farrago of doubts, fears, hopes, wishes, and all the flimsy furniture of a country miss's brain?

FAULKLAND. Ah! Jack, your heart and soul are not, like mine, fixed immutably on one only object. You throw for a large stake, but losing, you could stake and throw again: — but I have set my sum of happiness on this cast, and not to succeed, were to be stripped of all.

ABSOLUTE. But, for Heaven's sake! what grounds for 100 apprehension can your whimsical brain conjure up at present?

FAULKLAND. What grounds for apprehension, did you say? Heavens! are there not a thousand! I fear for her spirits — her health — her life. — My absence may fret her; her anxiety for my return, her fears for me may oppress her gentle temper: and for her health, does not every hour bring me cause to be alarmed? If it rains, some shower

---

l.81 reversion: *right of inheriting.*
l.87 forswear: *renounce.*
l.93 farrago: *a confused mixture.*

may even then have chilled her delicate frame! If the
110 wind be keen, some rude blast may have affected her!
The heat of noon, the dews of the evening, may endanger
the life of her, for whom only I value mine. O Jack! when
delicate and feeling souls are separated, there is not a
feature in the sky, not a movement of the elements, not
an aspiration of the breeze, but hints some cause for a
lover's apprehension!

ABSOLUTE. Ay, but we may choose whether we will take the
hint or not. — So, then, Faulkland, if you were convinced
that Julia were well and in spirits, you would be entirely
120 content?

FAULKLAND. I should be happy beyond measure — I am
anxious only for that.

ABSOLUTE. Then to cure your anxiety at once — Miss
Melville is in perfect health, and is at this moment in Bath.

FAULKLAND. Nay, Jack — don't trifle with me.

ABSOLUTE. She is arrived here with my father within this
hour.

FAULKLAND. Can you be serious?

ABSOLUTE. I thought you knew Sir Anthony better than to
130 be surprised at a sudden whim of this kind. — Seriously,
then, it is as I tell you — upon my honour.

FAULKLAND. My dear friend! — Hollo, Du-Peigne! my
hat. — My dear Jack — now nothing on earth can give me
a moment's uneasiness.

Re-enter FAG

FAG. Sir, Mr. Acres, just arrived, is below.

ABSOLUTE. Stay, Faulkland, this Acres lives within a mile
of Sir Anthony, and he shall tell you how your mistress has
been ever since you left her. — Fag, show the gentleman
up. [*Exit* FAG.

140 FAULKLAND. What, is he much acquainted in the family?

ABSOLUTE. Oh, very intimate: I insist on your not going:
besides, his character will divert you.

FAULKLAND. Well, I should like to ask him a few questions.

ABSOLUTE. He is likewise a rival of mine — that is, of my other self's, for he does not think his friend Captain Absolute ever saw the lady in question; and it is ridiculous enough to hear him complain to me of one Beverley, a concealed skulking rival, who, ——

FAULKLAND. Hush! — he's here.

Enter ACRES

ACRES. Ha! my dear friend, noble captain, and honest Jack, 150 how do'st thou? just arrived, faith, as you see. — Sir, your humble servant. — Warm work on the roads, Jack! — Odds whips and wheels! I've travelled like a comet, with a tail of dust all the way as long as the Mall.

ABSOLUTE. Ah! Bob, you are indeed an eccentric planet, but we know your attraction hither. — Give me leave to introduce Mr. Faulkland to you; Mr. Faulkland, Mr. Acres.

ACRES. Sir, I am most heartily glad to see you: sir, I solicit your connections. — Hey, Jack — what, this is Mr. 160 Faulkland, who ——

ABSOLUTE. Ay, Bob, Miss Melville's Mr. Faulkland.

ACRES. Odso! she and your father can be but just arrived before me: — I suppose you have seen them. Ah! Mr. Faulkland, you are indeed a happy man.

FAULKLAND. I have not seen Miss Melville yet, sir; — I hope she enjoyed full health and spirits in Devonshire?

ACRES. Never knew her better in my life, sir, — never better. Odds blushes and blooms! she has been as healthy as the German Spa. 170

FAULKLAND. Indeed! — I did hear that she had been a little indisposed.

---

l.154 the Mall: *the promenade in St. James's Park, London.*
l.170 Spa: *the word was applied to any locality where there are mineral springs with curative powers.*

ACRES. False, false, sir — only said to vex you: quite the reverse, I assure you.

FAULKLAND. There, Jack, you see she has the advantage of me; I had almost fretted myself ill.

ABSOLUTE. Now are you angry with your mistress for not having been sick?

FAULKLAND. No, no, you misunderstand me: yet surely a
180 little trifling indisposition is not an unnatural consequence of absence from those we love. — Now confess — isn't there something unkind in this violent, robust, unfeeling health?

ABSOLUTE. Oh, it was very unkind of her to be well in your absence, to be sure!

ACRES. Good apartments, Jack.

FAULKLAND. Well, sir, but you was saying that Miss Melville had been so exceedingly well — what, then, she has been merry and gay, I suppose? — Always in spirits —
190 hey?

ACRES. Merry, odds crickets! she has been the belle and spirit of the company wherever she has been — so lively and entertaining! so full of wit and humour!

FAULKLAND. There, Jack, there. — Oh, by my soul! there is an innate levity in woman, that nothing can overcome. — What! happy, and I away!

ABSOLUTE. Have done. — How foolish this is! just now you were only apprehensive for your mistress's spirits.

FAULKLAND. Why, Jack, have I been the joy and spirit of the
200 company?

ABSOLUTE. No indeed, you have not.

FAULKLAND. Have I been lively and entertaining?

ABSOLUTE. Oh, upon my word, I acquit you.

FAULKLAND. Have I been full of wit and humour?

ABSOLUTE. No, faith, to do you justice, you have been confoundedly stupid indeed.

ACRES. What's the matter with the gentleman?

ABSOLUTE. He is only expressing his great satisfaction at hearing that Julia has been so well and happy — that's all — hey, Faulkland? 210

FAULKLAND. Oh! I am rejoiced to hear it — yes, yes, she has a happy disposition!

ACRES. That she has indeed — Then she is so accomplished — so sweet a voice — so expert at her harpsichord — such a mistress of flat and sharp, squallante, rumblante, and quiverante! — There was this time month — odds minims and crochets! how she did chirrup at Mrs. Piano's concert!

FAULKLAND. There again, what say you to this? You see she has been all mirth and song — not a thought of me! 220

ABSOLUTE. Pho! man, is not music the food of love?

FAULKLAND. Well, well, it may be so. — Pray, Mr. —— , what's his name? — Do you remember what songs Miss Melville sung?

ACRES. Not I indeed.

ABSOLUTE. Stay, now, they were some pretty melancholy purling-stream airs, I warrant; perhaps you may recollect; — did she sing. *When absent from my soul's delight?*

ACRES. No, that wa'n't it.

ABSOLUTE. Or, *Go, gentle gales!*   [*Sings.* 230

ACRES. Oh, no! nothing like it. Odds! now I recollect one of them — *My heart's my own, my will is free.*   [*Sings.*

FAULKLAND. Fool! fool that I am! to fix all my happiness on such a trifler! 'Sdeath! to make herself the pipe and balladmonger of a circle! to soothe her light heart with catches and glees! — What can you say to this, sir?

---

l.214 harpsichord: *the keyboard instrument from which the piano was developed.*
l.221 is not music the food of love: '*If music be the food of love, play on.*' — Twelfth Night, *I. i. i.*
l.236 catches and glees: *types of song.*

ABSOLUTE. Why, that I should be glad to hear my mistress had been so merry, sir.

FAULKLAND. Nay, nay, nay — I'm not sorry that she has 240 been happy — no, no, I am glad of that — I would not have had her sad or sick — yet surely a sympathetic heart would have shown itself even in the choice of a song — she might have been temperately healthy, and somehow, plaintively gay; — but she has been dancing too, I doubt not!

ACRES. What does the gentleman say about dancing?

ABSOLUTE. He says the lady we speak of dances as well as she sings.

ACRES. Ay, truly, does she—there was at our last race ball——

250 FAULKLAND. There! — there — I told you so! I told you so! Oh! she thrives in my absence! — Dancing! but her whole feelings have been in opposition with mine; — I have been anxious, silent, pensive, sedentary — my days have been hours of care, my nights of watchfulness. — She has been all health! spirit! laugh! song! dance! —

ABSOLUTE. For Heaven's sake, Faulkland, don't expose yourself so! — Suppose she has danced, what then? — does not the ceremony of society often oblige ——

FAULKLAND. Well, well, I'll contain myself — perhaps as 260 you say — for form sake. — What, Mr. Acres, you were praising Miss Melville's manner of dancing a minuet — hey?

ACRES. Oh, I dare insure her for that — but what I was going to speak of was her country-dancing. Odds swimmings! she has such an air with her!

FAULKLAND. Now disappointment on her! — Defend this, Absolute; why don't you defend this? — Country-dances! jigs and reels! am I to blame now? A minuet I could have forgiven — I should not have minded that — I

l.261 minuet: *the most popular of the dances then fashionable.*

say I should not have regarded a minuet — but country- 270
dances! — Zounds! had she made one in a cotillon — I
believe I could have forgiven even that — but to be
monkey-led for a night! — to run the gauntlet through a
string of amorous palming puppies! — to show paces like
a managed filly! — Oh, Jack, there never can be but one
man in the world whom a truly modest and delicate
woman ought to pair with in a country-dance; and, even
then, the rest of the couples should be her great-uncles
and aunts!

ABSOLUTE. Ay, to be sure! — grandfathers and grand- 280
mothers!

FAULKLAND. If there be but one vicious mind in the set,
'twill spread like a contagion — the action of their pulse
beats to the lascivious movement of the jig — their quiver-
ing, warm-breathed sighs impregnate the very air — the
atmosphere becomes electrical to love, and each amorous
spark darts through every link of the chain! — I must
leave you — I own I am somewhat flurried — and that
confounded looby has perceived it. [*Going.*

ABSOLUTE. Nay, but stay, Faulkland, and thank Mr. Acres 290
for his good news.

FAULKLAND. Damn his news!

[*Exit.*

ABSOLUTE. Ha! ha! ha! poor Faulkland five minutes since —
'nothing on earth could give him a moment's uneasiness!'

ACRES. The gentleman wa'n't angry at my praising his mistress, was he?

ABSOLUTE. A little jealous, I believe, Bob.

ACRES. You don't say so? Ha! ha! jealous of me — that's a
good joke.

---

l.271 cotillon: *a quick French dance akin to the quadrille.*
l.275 a managed filly: *a young horse handled so as to show off its paces.*
l.289 looby: *lubber.*

300 ABSOLUTE. There's nothing strange in that, Bob; let me tell
you, that sprightly grace and insinuating manner of yours
will do some mischief among the girls here.

ACRES. Ah! you joke — ha! ha! mischief — ha! ha! but you
know I am not my own property, my dear Lydia has forestalled me. She could never abide me in the country,
because I used to dress so badly — but odds frogs and
tambours! I shan't take matters so here, now ancient
madam has no voice in it, I'll make my old clothes know
who's master. I shall straightway cashier the hunting-frock,
310 and render my leather breeches incapable. My hair has
been in training some time.

ABSOLUTE. Indeed!

ACRES. Ay — and thoff the side curls are a little restive, my
hind-part takes it very kindly.

ABSOLUTE. Oh, you'll polish, I doubt not.

ACRES. Absolutely I propose so — then if I can find out this
Ensign Beverley, odds triggers and flints! I'll make him
know the difference o't.

ABSOLUTE. Spoke like a man! But pray, Bob, I observe you
320 have got an odd kind of a new method of swearing ——

ACRES. Ha! ha! you've taken notice of it — 'tis genteel,
isn't it? — I didn't invent it myself though; but a commander in our militia, a great scholar, I assure you, says
that there is no meaning in the common oaths, and that
nothing but their antiquity makes them respectable; —
because, he says, the ancients would never stick to an oath
or two, but would say, by Jove! or by Bacchus! or by
Mars! or by Venus! or by Pallas! according to the sentiment: so that to swear with propriety, says my little
330 major, the oath should be an echo to the sense; and this

l.306 frogs: *a form of cloak button.*
l.307 tambours: *a frame for embroidery.*
l.313 thoff: *though.*
ll.328-9 sentiment: *i.e. the toast, the sense.*

we call the *oath referential* or *sentimental swearing* — ha! ha! 'tis genteel, isn't it?

ABSOLUTE. Very genteel, and very new, indeed! — and I dare say will supplant all other figures of imprecation.

ACRES. Ay, ay, the best terms will grow obsolete — Damns have had their day.

Re-enter FAG

FAG. Sir, there is a gentleman below desires to see you. — Shall I show him into the parlour?

ABSOLUTE. Ay, you may.

ACRES. Well, I must be gone —— 340

ABSOLUTE. Stay; who is it, Fag?

FAG. Your father, sir.

ABSOLUTE. You puppy, why didn't you show him up directly?   [*Exit* FAG.

ACRES. You have business with Sir Anthony. — I expect a message from Mrs. Malaprop at my lodgings. I have sent also to my dear friend Sir Lucius O'Trigger. Adieu, Jack! we must meet at night, when you shall give me a dozen bumpers to little Lydia.

ABSOLUTE. That I will with all my heart. — [*Exit* ACRES.] 350 Now for a parental lecture — I hope he has heard nothing of the business that has brought me here — I wish the gout had held him fast in Devonshire, with all my soul!

Enter SIR ANTHONY ABSOLUTE

Sir, I am delighted to see you here, looking so well! your sudden arrival at Bath made me apprehensive for your health.

SIR ANTHONY. Very apprehensive, I dare say, Jack. — What, you are recruiting here, hey?

---

l.331 sentimental: *elevated*.
l.334 imprecation: *swearing*.
l.349 bumper: *a glass filled to the brim for a toast*.

ABSOLUTE. Yes, sir, I am on duty.

360 SIR ANTHONY. Well, Jack, I am glad to see you, though I did not expect it, for I was going to write to you on a little matter of business. — Jack, I have been considering that I grow old and infirm, and shall probably not trouble you long.

ABSOLUTE. Pardon me, sir, I never saw you look more strong and hearty; and I pray frequently that you may continue so.

SIR ANTHONY. I hope your prayers may be heard, with all my heart. Well then, Jack, I have been considering that I
370 am so strong and hearty I may continue to plague you a long time. Now, Jack, I am sensible that the income of your commission, and what I have hitherto allowed you, is but a small pittance for a lad of your spirit.

ABSOLUTE. Sir, you are very good.

SIR ANTHONY. And it is my wish, while yet I live, to have my boy make some figure in the world. I have resolved, therefore, to fix you at once in a noble independence.

ABSOLUTE. Sir, your kindness overpowers me — such generosity makes the gratitude of reason more lively than
380 the sensations even of filial affection.

SIR ANTHONY. I am glad you are so sensible of my attention — and you shall be master of a large estate in a few weeks.

ABSOLUTE. Let my future life, sir, speak my gratitude; I cannot express the sense I have of your munificence. — Yet, sir, I presume you would not wish me to quit the army?

SIR ANTHONY. Oh, that shall be as your wife chooses.

ABSOLUTE. My wife, sir!

SIR ANTHONY. Ay, ay, settle that between you — settle that between you.

390 ABSOLUTE. A wife, sir, did you say?

1.381 sensible: *appreciative.*

SIR ANTHONY. Ay, a wife — why, did not I mention her before?

ABSOLUTE. Not a word of her, sir.

SIR ANTHONY. Odd so! — I mustn't forget her though. — Yes, Jack, the independence I was talking of is by a marriage — the fortune is saddled with a wife — but I suppose that makes no difference.

ABSOLUTE. Sir! sir! — you amaze me!

SIR ANTHONY. Why, what's the matter with the fool? Just now you were all gratitude and duty. 400

ABSOLUTE. I was, sir, — you talked to me of independence and a fortune, but not a word of a wife.

SIR ANTHONY. Why — what difference does that make? Odds life, sir! if you have the estate you must take it with the live stock on it, as it stands.

ABSOLUTE. If my happiness is to be the price, I must beg leave to decline the purchase. — Pray, sir, who is the lady?

SIR ANTHONY. What's that to you, sir? — Come, give me your promise to love, and to marry her directly.

ABSOLUTE. Sure, sir, this is not very reasonable, to summon 410 my affections for a lady I know nothing of!

SIR ANTHONY. I am sure, sir, 'tis more unreasonable in you to object to a lady you know nothing of.

ABSOLUTE. Then, sir, I must tell you plainly that my inclinations are fixed on another — my heart is engaged to an angel.

SIR ANTHONY. Then pray let it send an excuse. It is very sorry — but business prevents its waiting on her.

ABSOLUTE. But my vows are pledged to her.

SIR ANTHONY. Let her foreclose, Jack; let her foreclose; 420 they are not worth redeeming; besides, you have the

---

l.420 foreclose: *to deprive one who has mortgaged his property of the right of redeeming it.*

angel's vows in exchange, I suppose; so there can be no
loss there.

ABSOLUTE. You must excuse me, sir, if I tell you, once for
all, that in this point I cannot obey you.

SIR ANTHONY. Hark'ee, Jack; I have heard you for some
time with patience — I have been cool — quite cool; but
take care — you know I am compliance itself — when I
am not thwarted; — no one more easily led — when I
430 have my own way; — but don't put me in a frenzy.

ABSOLUTE. Sir, I must repeat it — in this I cannot obey you.

SIR ANTHONY. Now damn me! if ever I call you Jack again
while I live!

ABSOLUTE. Nay, sir, but hear me.

SIR ANTHONY. Sir, I won't hear a word — not a word! not
one word! so give me your promise by a nod — and I'll
tell you what, Jack—I mean, you dog—if you don't, by ——

ABSOLUTE. What, sir, promise to link myself to some mass
of ugliness! to —

440 SIR ANTHONY. Zounds! sirrah! the lady shall be as ugly as
I choose: she shall have a lump on each shoulder; she
shall be as crooked as the crescent; her one eye shall roll
like the bull's in Cox's Museum; she shall have a skin like
a mummy, and the beard of a Jew — she shall be all this,
sirrah! — yet I will make you ogle her all day, and sit up
all night to write sonnets on her beauty.

ABSOLUTE. This is reason and moderation indeed!

SIR ANTHONY. None of your sneering, puppy! no grinning,
jackanapes!

450 ABSOLUTE. Indeed, sir, I never was in a worse humour for
mirth in my life.

---

l.442 the crescent: *the moon in her first quarter*.
l.443 Cox's Museum: *an exhibition of curiosities open at the time in
Bond Street, London.*

SIR ANTHONY. 'Tis false, sir, I know you are laughing in your sleeve; I know you'll grin when I am gone, sirrah!

ABSOLUTE. Sir, I hope I know my duty better.

SIR ANTHONY. None of your passion, sir! none of your violence, if you please! — It won't do with me, I promise you.

ABSOLUTE. Indeed, sir, I never was cooler in my life.

SIR ANTHONY. 'Tis a confounded lie! — I know you are in a passion in your heart; I know you are, you hypocritical 460 young dog! but it won't do.

ABSOLUTE. Nay, sir, upon my word ——

SIR ANTHONY. So you will fly out! can't you be cool like me? What the devil good can passion do? — Passion is of no service, you impudent, insolent, overbearing reprobate! — There, you sneer again! don't provoke me! — but you rely upon the mildness of my temper — you do, you dog! you play upon the meekness of my disposition! — Yet take care — the patience of a saint may be overcome at last! — but mark! I give you six hours and a half to con- 470 sider of this: if you then agree, without any condition, to do everything on earth that I choose, why — confound you! I may in time forgive you. — If not, zounds! don't enter the same hemisphere with me! don't dare to breathe the same air, or use the same light with me; but get an atmosphere and a sun of your own! I'll strip you of your commission; I'll lodge a five-and-three-pence in the hands of trustees, and you shall live on the interest. — I'll disown you, I'll disinherit you, I'll unget you! and damn me! if ever I call you Jack again! [Exit. 480

ABSOLUTE. Mild, gentle, considerate father — I kiss your hands! What a tender method of giving his opinion in these matters Sir Anthony has! I dare not trust him with the truth. — I wonder what old wealthy hag it is that he

l.477 I'll lodge a five-and-three-pence, etc.: the same idea as 'I'll cut you off with a shilling'.

wants to bestow on me! — Yet he married himself for love! and was in his youth a bold intriguer, and a gay companion!

Re-enter FAG

FAG. Assuredly, sir, your father is wrath to a degree; he comes downstairs eight or ten steps at a time — muttering, 490 growling, and thumping the banisters all the way: I and the cook's dog stand bowing at the door — rap! he gives me a stroke on the head with his cane; bids me carry that to my master; then kicking the poor turnspit into the area, damns us all, for a puppy triumvirate! — Upon my credit, sir, were I in your place, and found my father such very bad company, I should certainly drop his acquaintance.

ABSOLUTE. Cease your impertinence, sir, at present. — Did you come in for nothing more? — Stand out of the way!
[*Pushes him aside and exit.*

FAG. So! Sir Anthony trims my master: he is afraid to 500 reply to his father — then vents his spleen on poor Fag! When one is vexed by one person, to revenge one's self on another, who happens to come in the way, is the vilest injustice! Ah! it shows the worst temper—the basest——

Enter BOY

BOY. Mr. Fag; Mr. Fag! your master calls you.

FAG. Well, you little dirty puppy, you need not bawl so! — The meanest disposition! the ——

BOY. Quick, quick, Mr. Fag!

FAG. Quick! quick! you impudent jackanapes! am I to be commanded by you too? you little impertinent, insolent, 510 kitchen-bred ——

[*Exit kicking and beating him.*

---

l.493 turnspit: *a small breed of dog formerly employed on a treadmill wheel to turn a spit on which meat was roasted.*
l.499 trims: *rebukes.*

Scene II. *The North Parade*

Enter LUCY

LUCY. So — I shall have another rival to add to my mistress's list — Captain Absolute. However, I shall not enter his name till my purse has received notice in form. Poor Acres is dismissed! — Well, I have done him a last friendly office, in letting him know that Beverley was here before him. — Sir Lucius is generally more punctual, when he expects to hear from his *dear Dalia*, as he calls her: I wonder he's not here! — I have a little scruple of conscience from this deceit; though I should not be paid so well, if my hero knew that Delia was near fifty, and her own mis- 10 tress.

Enter SIR LUCIUS O'TRIGGER

SIR LUCIUS. Ha! my little ambassadress — upon my conscience, I have been looking for you; I have been on the South Parade this half hour.

LUCY [*speaking simply*]. O gemini! and I have been waiting for your worship here on the North.

SIR LUCIUS. Faith! — may be that was the reason we did not meet; and it is very comical too, how you could go out and I not see you — for I was only taking a nap at the Parade Coffee-house, and I chose the window on purpose that I 20 might not miss you.

LUCY. My stars! Now I'd wager a sixpence I went by while you were asleep.

SIR LUCIUS. Sure enough it must have been so — and I never dreamt it was so late, till I waked. Well, but my little girl, have you got nothing for me?

LUCY. Yes, but I have — I've got a letter for you in my pocket.

1.14 the South Parade: *The North and South Parades, then, as now, a central attraction of Bath.*

SIR LUCIUS. O faith! I guessed you weren't come empty-
30   handed. — Well — let me see what the dear creature says.

LUCY. There, Sir Lucius.   [*Gives him a letter.*

SIR LUCIUS. [*Reads.*] *Sir — there is often a sudden incentive
impulse in love, that has a greater induction than years of
domestic combination: such was the commotion I felt at the
first superfluous view of Sir Lucius O'Trigger.* — Very
pretty, upon my word. — *Female punctuation forbids me to
say more, yet let me add, that it will give me joy infallible to
find Sir Lucius worthy the last criterion of my affections.*
                           DELIA.

40   Upon my conscience! Lucy, your lady is a great mistress of
language. Faith, she's quite the queen of the dictionary! —
for the devil a word dare refuse coming at her call —
though one would think it was quite out of hearing.

LUCY. Ay, sir, a lady of her experience ——

SIR LUCIUS. Experience! what, at seventeen?

LUCY. O true, sir — but then she reads so — my stars! how
she will read off hand!

SIR LUCIUS. Faith, she must be very deep read to write this
way — though she is rather an arbitrary writer too — for
50   here are a great many poor words pressed into the service
of this note, that would get their *habeas corpus* from any
court in Christendom.

LUCY. Ah! Sir Lucius, if you were to hear how she talks of
you!

SIR LUCIUS. Oh, tell her I'll make her the best husband in
the world, and Lady O'Trigger into the bargain. — But
we must get the old gentlewoman's consent — and do
everything fairly.

LUCY. Nay, Sir Lucius, I thought you wa'n't rich enough to
60   be so nice!

---

l.51 habeas corpus: *An Act, compelling judges to have the person*
(corpus) *of a prisoner brought into court for trial.*
l.60 nice: *punctilious.*

SIR LUCIUS. Upon my word, young woman, you have hit it:
— I am so poor, that I can't afford to do a dirty action. — If
I did not want money, I'd steal your mistress and her
fortune with a great deal of pleasure. — However, my
pretty girl, [*Gives her money,*] here's a little something to
buy you a ribbon; and meet me in the evening, and I'll give
you an answer to this. So, hussy, take a kiss beforehand to
put you in mind.

[*Kisses her.*

LUCY. O Lud! Sir Lucius — I never seed such a gemman!
My lady won't like you if you're so impudent.   70

SIR LUCIUS. Faith she will, Lucy! — That same — pho!
what's the name of it? — modesty — is a quality in a lover
more praised by the women than liked; so, if your mistress
asks you whether Sir Lucius ever gave you a kiss, tell her
fifty — my dear.

LUCY. What, would you have me tell her a lie?

SIR LUCIUS. Ah, then, you baggage! I'll make it a truth
presently.

LUCY. For shame now! here is someone coming.

SIR LUCIUS. Oh, faith, I'll quiet your conscience!   80

[*Exit, humming a tune.*

Enter FAG

FAG. So, so, ma'am! I humbly beg pardon.

LUCY. O Lud! now, Mr. Fag — you flurry one so.

FAG. Come, come, Lucy, here's no one by — so a little less
simplicity, with a grain or two more sincerity, if you please.
— You play false with us, madam — and I saw you give the
baronet a letter. My master shall know this — and if he
don't call him out, I will.

---

l.69 gemman: *gentleman.*
l.87 call him out: *to a duel.*

LUCY. Ha! ha! ha! you gentlemen's gentlemen are so hasty.
— That letter was from Mrs. Malaprop, simpleton. — She
90 is taken with Sir Lucius's address.

FAG. How! what tastes some people have! — Why, I suppose
I have walked by her window a hundred times. — But
what says our young lady? any message to my master?

LUCY. Sad news, Mr. Fag. — A worse rival than Acres ! Sir
Anthony Absolute has proposed his son.

FAG. What, Captain Absolute?

LUCY. Even so — I overheard it all.

FAG. Ha! ha! ha! very good, faith. Good-bye, Lucy, I must
away with this news.

100 LUCY. Well, you may laugh — but it is true, I assure you. —
[*Going.*] But, Mr. Fag, tell your master not to be cast down
by this.

FAG. Oh, he'll be so disconsolate!

LUCY. And charge him not to think of quarrelling with
young Absolute!

FAG. Never fear! never fear!

LUCY. Be sure — bid him keep up his spirits.

FAG. We will — we will.   [*Exeunt severally.*

ACT III

Scene I. *The North Parade*

Enter CAPTAIN ABSOLUTE

ABSOLUTE. 'Tis just as Fag told me, indeed. Whimsical
enough, faith! My father wants to force me to marry the
very girl I am plotting to run away with! He must not
know of my connection with her yet awhile. He has too
summary a method of proceeding in these matters. However, I'll read my recantation instantly. My conversion is

---

I.88 gentleman's gentleman: *valet.*

something sudden, indeed — but I can assure him it is very sincere. So, so — here he comes. He looks plaguy gruff. [*Steps aside.*

Enter SIR ANTHONY ABSOLUTE

SIR ANTHONY. No. — I'll die sooner than forgive him. Die, 10 did I say? I'll live these fifty years to plague him. At our last meeting, his impudence had almost put me out of temper. An obstinate, passionate, self-willed boy! Who can he take after? This is my return for getting him before all his brothers and sisters! — for putting him, at twelve years old, into a marching regiment, and allowing him fifty pounds a year, besides his pay, ever since! But I have done with him; he's anybody's son for me. I never will see him more, never — never — never.

ABSOLUTE. [*Aside, coming forward*]. Now for a penitential 20 face.

SIR ANTHONY. Fellow, get out of my way!

ABSOLUTE. Sir, you see a penitent before you.

SIR ANTHONY. I see an impudent scoundrel before me.

ABSOLUTE. A sincere penitent. I am come, sir, to acknowledge my error, and to submit entirely to your will.

SIR ANTHONY. What's that?

ABSOLUTE. I have been revolving, and reflecting and considering on your past goodness, and kindness, and condescension to me. 30

SIR ANTHONY. Well, sir?

ABSOLUTE. I have been likewise weighing and balancing what you were pleased to mention concerning duty, and obedience, and authority.

SIR ANTHONY. Well, puppy?

ABSOLUTE. Why then, sir, the result of my reflections is — a resolution to sacrifice every inclination of my own to your satisfaction.

---

l.16 a marching regiment: *one liable to be ordered abroad.*

SIR ANTHONY. Why now you talk sense — absolute sense —
40 I never heard anything more sensible in my life. Confound you! you shall be Jack again.

ABSOLUTE. I am happy in the appellation.

SIR ANTHONY. Why then, Jack, my dear Jack, I will now inform you who the lady really is. Nothing but your passion and violence, you silly fellow, prevented my telling you at first. Prepare, Jack, for wonder and rapture — prepare. What think you of Miss Lydia Languish?

ABSOLUTE. Languish! What, the Languishes of Worcestershire?

50 SIR ANTHONY. Worcestershire! No. Did you never meet Mrs. Malaprop and her niece, Miss Languish, who came into our country just before you were last ordered to your regiment?

ABSOLUTE. Malaprop! Languish! I don't remember ever to have heard the names before. Yet, stay — I think I do recollect something. Languish! Languish! She squints, don't she? A little red-haired girl?

SIR ANTHONY. Squints! A red-haired girl! Zounds! No.

ABSOLUTE. Then I must have forgot; it can't be the same
60 person.

SIR ANTHONY. Jack! Jack! what think you of blooming, love-breathing seventeen?

ABSOLUTE. As to that, sir, I am quite indifferent. If I can please you in the matter, 'tis all I desire.

SIR ANTHONY. Nay, but Jack, such eyes! such eyes! so innocently wild! so bashfully irresolute! not a glance but speaks and kindles some thought of love! Then, Jack, her cheeks! her cheeks, Jack! so deeply blushing at the insinuations of her tell-tale eyes! Then, Jack, her lips! O
70 Jack, lips smiling at their own discretion; and if not smiling, more sweetly pouting; more lovely in sullenness!

---

l.42 appellation: *name.*

ABSOLUTE. [*Aside*]. That's she indeed. Well done, old gentleman.

SIR ANTHONY. Then, Jack, her neck! O Jack! Jack!

ABSOLUTE. And which is to be mine, sir, the niece, or the aunt?

SIR ANTHONY. Why, you unfeeling, insensible puppy, I despise you! When I was of your age, such a description would have made me fly like a rocket! The aunt indeed! Odds life! when I ran away with your mother, I would not 80 have touched anything old or ugly to gain an empire.

ABSOLUTE. Not to please your father, sir?

SIR ANTHONY. To please my father! zounds! not to please — Oh, my father — odd so! — yes — yes; if my father indeed had desired — that's quite another matter. Though he wa'n't the indulgent father that I am, Jack.

ABSOLUTE. I dare say not, sir.

SIR ANTHONY. But, Jack, you are not sorry to find your mistress is so beautiful?

ABSOLUTE. Sir, I repeat it — if I please you in this affair, 90 'tis all I desire. Not that I think a woman the worse for being handsome; but, sir, if you please to recollect, you before hinted something about a hump or two, one eye, and a few more graces of that kind — now, without being very nice, I own I should rather choose a wife of mine to have the usual number of limbs, and limited quantity of back; and though one eye may be very agreeable, yet as the prejudice has always run in favour of two, I would not wish to affect a singularity in that article.

SIR ANTHONY. What a phlegmatic sot it is! Why, sirrah, 100 you're an anchorite! — a vile, insensible stock. You a soldier! — you're a walking block, fit only to dust the company's regimentals on! Odds life! I have a great mind to marry the girl myself.

---

l.101 anchorite: *a religious recluse*; stock: *block of wood*.
l.103 regimentals: *uniform*.

ABSOLUTE. I am entirely at your disposal, sir: if you should think of addressing Miss Languish yourself, I suppose you would have me marry the aunt; or if you should change your mind, and take the old lady — 'tis the same to me — I'll marry the niece.

110 SIR ANTHONY. Upon my word, Jack, thou'rt either a very great hypocrite, or — but, come, I know your indifference on such a subject must be all a lie — I'm sure it must —come, now—come, confess Jack—you have been lying— ha'n't you? You have been playing the hypocrite, hey! — I'll never forgive you, if you ha'n't been lying and playing the hypocrite.

ABSOLUTE. I'm sorry, sir, that the respect and duty which I bear to you should be so mistaken.

SIR ANTHONY. Hang your respect and duty! But come 120 along with me, I'll write a note to Mrs. Malaprop, and you shall visit the lady directly. Her eyes shall be the Promethean torch to you — come along, I'll never forgive you, if you don't come back stark mad with rapture and impatience — if you don't, egad, I will marry the girl myself! [*Exeunt*.

SCENE II. *Julia's Dressing-room*

FAULKLAND *discovered alone*

FAULKLAND. They told me Julia would return directly; I wonder she is not yet come! How mean does this captious, unsatisfied temper of mine appear to my cooler judgment! Yet I know not that I indulge it in any other point: but on this one subject, and to this one subject, whom I think I love beyond my life, I am ever ungenerously fretful and madly capricious! I am conscious of it — yet I cannot correct myself! What tender honest joy sparkled in her eyes

---

ll.121-2 the Promethean torch: *Prometheus stole the secret of fire from heaven in order to endow man with life.*

when we met! how delicate was the warmth of her expres-
sions! I was ashamed to appear less happy — though I had 10
come resolved to wear a face of coolness and upbraiding.
Sir Anthony's presence prevented my proposed expostula-
tions: Yet I must be satisfied that she has not been so very
happy in my absence. She is coming! Yes! — I know the
nimbleness of her tread, when she thinks her impatient
Faulkland counts the moments of her stay.

Enter JULIA

JULIA. I had not hoped to see you again so soon.

FAULKLAND. Could I, Julia, be contented with my first
welcome — restrained as we were by the presence of a
third person?   20

JULIA. O Faulkland, when your kindness can make me thus
happy, let me not think that I discovered something of
coldness in your first salutation.

FAULKLAND. 'Twas but your fancy, Julia. I was rejoiced to
see you — to see you in such health. Sure I had no cause
for coldness?

JULIA. Nay then, I see you have taken something ill. You
must not conceal from me what it is.

FAULKLAND. Well, then — shall I own to you that my joy at
hearing of your health and arrival here, by your neighbour 30
Acres, was somewhat damped by his dwelling much on the
high spirits you had enjoyed in Devonshire — on your
mirth — your singing — dancing — and I know not what!
For such is my temper, Julia, that I should regard every
mirthful moment in your absence as a treason to constancy. The mutual tear that steals down the cheek of
parting lovers is a compact, that no smile shall live there
till they meet again.

JULIA. Must I never cease to tax my Faulkland with this
teasing minute caprice? Can the idle reports of a silly boor 40
weigh in your breast against my tried affection?

FAULKLAND. They have no weight with me, Julia: No, no —
I am happy if you have been so — yet only say, that you
did not sing with mirth — say that you thought of Faulkland in the dance.

JULIA. I never can be happy in your absence. If I wear a
countenance of content, it is to show that my mind holds
no doubt of my Faulkland's truth. If I seemed sad, it were
to make malice triumph; and say, that I had fixed my
50 heart on one, who left me to lament his roving, and my
own credulity. Believe me, Faulkland, I mean not to upbraid you, when I say, that I have often dressed sorrow in
smiles, lest my friends should guess whose unkindness had
caused my tears.

FAULKLAND. You were ever all goodness to me. Oh, I am a
brute, when I but admit a doubt of your true constancy!

JULIA. If ever without such cause from you, as I will not
suppose possible, you find my affections veering but a
point, may I become a proverbial scoff for levity and base
60 ingratitude.

FAULKLAND. Ah! Julia, that last word is grating to me. I
would I had no title to your gratitude! Search your heart,
Julia; perhaps what you have mistaken for love, is but the
warm effusion of a too thankful heart.

JULIA. For what quality must I love you?

FAULKLAND. For no quality! To regard me for any quality
of mind or understanding, were only to esteem me. And
for person — I have often wished myself deformed, to be
convinced that I owed no obligation there for any part of
70 your affection.

JULIA. Where nature has bestowed a show of nice attention
in the features of a man, he should laugh at it as mis-
placed. I have seen men, who in this vain article, perhaps,
might rank above you; but my heart has never asked my
eyes if it were so or not.

l.71 a show of nice attention ... *made some one outwardly attractive.*

FAULKLAND. Now this is not well from you, Julia — I despise person in a man — yet if you loved me as I wish, though I were an Ethiop, you'd think none so fair.

JULIA. I see you are determined to be unkind! The contract which my poor father bound us in gives you more than a 80 lover's privilege.

FAULKLAND. Again, Julia, you raise ideas that feed and justify my doubts. I would not have been more free — no — I am proud of my restraint. Yet — yet — perhaps your high respect alone for this solemn compact has fettered your inclinations, which else had made a worthier choice. How shall I be sure, had you remained unbound in thought and promise, that I should still have been the object of your persevering love?

JULIA. Then try me now. Let us be free as strangers as to 90 what is past: my heart will not feel more liberty!

FAULKLAND. There now! so hasty, Julia! so anxious to be free! If your love for me were fixed and ardent, you would not lose your hold, even though I wished it!

JULIA. Oh! you torture me to the heart! I cannot bear it.

FAULKLAND. I do not mean to distress you. If I loved you less I should never give you an uneasy moment. But hear me. All my fretful doubts arise from this. Women are not used to weigh and separate the motives of their affections: the cold dictates of prudence, gratitude, or filial duty, may 100 sometimes be mistaken for the pleadings of the heart. I would not boast — yet let me say, that I have neither age, person, nor character, to found dislike on; my fortune such as few ladies could be charged with indiscretion in the match. O Julia! when love receives such countenance from prudence, nice minds will be suspicious of its birth.

JULIA. I know not whither your insinuations would tend: — but as they seem pressing to insult me, I will spare you the

---

l.77 person: *outward good looks.*
l.78 an Ethiop: *the term applied generally to any negro.*

110 regret of having done so. — I have given you no cause for this! [*Exit in tears.*

FAULKLAND. In tears! Stay, Julia: stay but for a moment. — The door is fastened! — Julia! — my soul — but for one moment! — I hear her sobbing! — 'Sdeath! what a brute am I to use her thus! Yet stay. — Ay — she is coming now: — how little resolution there is in woman! — how a few soft words can turn them! — No, faith! — she is not coming either. — Why, Julia — my love — say but that you forgive me — come but to tell me that — now this is being too resentful. Stay! she is coming too — I thought 120 she would — no steadiness in anything: her going away must have been a mere trick then — she *sha'n't* see that I was hurt by it. — I'll affect indifference — [*Hums a tune: then listens.*] No — zounds! she's not coming! — nor don't intend it, I suppose. — This is not steadiness, but obstinacy! Yet I deserve it. — What, after so long an absence to quarrel with her tenderness! — 'twas barbarous and unmanly! — I should be ashamed to see her now. — I'll wait till her just resentment is abated — and when I distress her so again, may I lose her for ever, and 130 be linked instead to some antique virago, whose gnawing passions, and long hoarded spleen, shall make me curse my folly half the day and all the night! [*Exit.*

Scene III. *Mrs. Malaprop's Lodgings*

MRS. MALAPROP, *with a letter in her hand, and* CAPTAIN ABSOLUTE

MRS. MALAPROP. Your being Sir Anthony's son, captain, would itself be a sufficient accommodation; but from the ingenuity of your appearance, I am convinced you deserve the character here given of you.

ABSOLUTE. Permit me to say, madam, that as I never yet have had the pleasure of seeing Miss Languish, my principal inducement in this affair at present is the honour of

---

l.130 virago: *a turbulent woman, vixen.*

being allied to Mrs. Malaprop; of whose intellectual accomplishments, elegant manners, and unaffected learning, no tongue is silent.   10

MRS. MALAPROP. Sir, you do me infinite honour! I beg, captain, you'll be seated. — [*They sit.*] Ah! few gentlemen, now-a-days, know how to value the ineffectual qualities in a woman! few think how a little knowledge becomes a gentlewoman! — Men have no sense now but for the worthless flower of beauty!

ABSOLUTE. It is but too true, indeed, ma'am; — yet I fear our ladies should share the blame — they think our admiration of beauty so great, that knowledge in them would be superfluous. Thus, like garden-trees, they seldom show 20 fruit, till time has robbed them of the more specious blossom. — Few, like Mrs. Malaprop and the orange-tree, are rich in both at once.

MRS. MALAPROP. Sir, you overpower me with good-breeding. — He is the very pine-apple of politeness! — You are not ignorant, captain, that this giddy girl has somehow contrived to fix her affections on a beggarly, strolling, eavesdropping ensign, whom none of us have seen, and nobody knows anything of.

ABSOLUTE. Oh, I have heard the silly affair before. — I'm 30 not at all prejudiced against her on that account.

MRS. MALAPROP. You are very good and very considerate, captain. I am sure I have done everything in my power since I exploded the affair; long ago I laid my positive conjunctions on her, never to think on the fellow again; — I have since laid Sir Anthony's preposition before her; but, I am sorry to say, she seems resolved to decline every particle that I enjoin her.

ABSOLUTE. It must be very distressing, indeed, ma'am.

MRS. MALAPROP. Oh! it gives me the hydrostatics to such a 40 degree! — I thought she had persisted from corresponding with him; but, behold, this very day, I have interceded another letter from the fellow; I believe I have it in my pocket.

ABSOLUTE. [*Aside*]. Oh, the devil! my last note.

MRS. MALAPROP. Ay, here it is.

ABSOLUTE. [*Aside*]. Ay, my note indeed! O the little traitress Lucy.

MRS. MALAPROP. There, perhaps you may know the writing. [*Gives him the letter.*]

ABSOLUTE. I think I have seen the hand before — yes, I certainly must have seen this hand before —

MRS. MALAPROP. Nay, but read it, captain.

ABSOLUTE [*Reads*]. *My soul's idol, my adored Lydia!* — Very tender indeed!

MRS. MALAPROP. Tender! ay, and profane too, o' my conscience.

ABSOLUTE [*Reads*]. *I am excessively alarmed at the intelligence you send me, the more so as my new rival* ——

MRS. MALAPROP. That's you, sir.

ABSOLUTE [*Reads*]. *Has universally the character of being an accomplished gentleman and a man of honour.* Well, that's handsome enough.

MRS. MALAPROP. Oh, the fellow has some design in writing so.

ABSOLUTE. That he had, I'll answer for him, ma'am.

MRS. MALAPROP. But go on, sir — you'll see presently.

ABSOLUTE [*Reads*]. *As for the old weather-beaten she-dragon who guards you* — Who can he mean by that?

MRS. MALAPROP. Me, sir! — me! — he means me! — There — what do you think now? — but go on a little further.

---

l.56 profane: *immodest.*

ABSOLUTE. Impudent scoundrel! — [*Reads*]. *it shall go hard but I will elude her vigilance, as I am told that the same ridiculous vanity, which makes her dress up her coarse features, and deck her dull chat with hard words which she don't understand* ——

MRS. MALAPROP. There, sir, an attack upon my language! what do you think of that? — an aspersion upon my parts of speech! was ever such a brute! Sure, if I reprehend anything in this world, it is the use of my oracular tongue, and a nice derangement of epitaphs! 80

ABSOLUTE. He deserves to be hanged and quartered! Let me see — [*Reads.*] *same ridiculous vanity* ——

MRS. MALAPROP. You need not read it again, sir.

ABSOLUTE. I beg pardon, ma'am. — [*Reads.*] *does also lay her open to the grossest deceptions from flattery and pretended admiration* — an impudent coxcomb! — *so that I have a scheme to see you shortly with the old harridan's consent, and even to make her a go-between in our interview.* — Was ever such assurance! 90

MRS. MALAPROP. Did you ever hear anything like it? — he'll elude my vigilance, will he — yes, yes! ha! ha! he's very likely to enter these doors; we'll try who can plot best!

ABSOLUTE. So we will, ma'am — so we will! Ha! ha! ha! a conceited puppy, ha! ha! ha! — Well, but, Mrs. Malaprop, as the girl seems so infatuated by this fellow, suppose you were to wink at her corresponding with him for a little time — let her even plot an elopement with him — then do you connive at her escape — while I, just in the 100 nick, will have the fellow laid by the heels, and fairly contrive to carry her off in his stead.

MRS. MALAPROP. I am delighted with the scheme; never was anything better perpetrated!

---

l.87 coxcomb: *an impudent fellow.*
l.88 harridan: *hag.*

ABSOLUTE. But, pray, could not I see the lady for a few minutes now? — I should like to try her temper a little.

MRS. MALAPROP. Why, I don't know — I doubt she is not prepared for a visit of this kind. There is a decorum in these matters.

110 ABSOLUTE. O Lord! she won't mind me — only tell her Beverley ——

MRS. MALAPROP. Sir!

ABSOLUTE. [*Aside*]. Gently, good tongue.

MRS. MALAPROP. What did you say of Beverley?

ABSOLUTE. Oh, I was going to propose that you should tell her, by way of jest, that it was Beverley who was below; she'd come down fast enough then — ha! ha! ha!

MRS. MALAPROP. 'Twould be a trick she well deserves; besides, you know the fellow tells her he'll get my consent
120 to see her — ha! ha! Let him if he can, I say again. Lydia, come down here!—[*Calling*.] He'll make me a go-between in their interviews! — ha! ha! ha! Come down, I say, Lydia! I don't wonder at your laughing, ha! ha! ha! his impudence is truly ridiculous.

ABSOLUTE. 'Tis very ridiculous, upon my soul, ma'am, ha! ha! ha!

MRS. MALAPROP. The little hussy won't hear. Well, I'll go and tell her at once who it is — she shall know that Captain Absolute is come to wait on her. And I'll make her
130 behave as becomes a young woman.

ABSOLUTE. As you please, ma'am.

MRS. MALAPROP. For the present, captain, your servant. Ah! you've not done laughing yet, I see — elude my vigilance; yes, yes; ha! ha! ha! [*Exit*.

ABSOLUTE. Ha! ha! ha! one would think now that I might throw off all disguise at once, and seize my prize with security; but such is Lydia's caprice, that to undeceive were probably to lose her. I'll see whether she knows me. [*Walks aside, and seems engaged in looking at the pictures.*

Enter LYDIA

LYDIA. What a scene am I now to go through! surely nothing can be more dreadful than to be obliged to listen to the 140 loathsome addresses of a stranger to one's heart. I have heard of girls persecuted as I am, who have appealed in behalf of their favoured lover to the generosity of his rival; suppose I were to try it — there stands the hated rival — an officer too! — but oh, how unlike my Beverley! I wonder he don't begin — truly he seems a very negligent wooer! — quite at his ease, upon my word! — I'll speak first — Mr. Absolute.

ABSOLUTE. Ma'am.   [*Turns round.*

LYDIA. O heavens! Beverley!   150

ABSOLUTE. Hush! — hush, my life! softly! be not surprised!

LYDIA. I am so astonished! and so terrified! and so over-joyed! — for Heaven's sake! how came you here?

ABSOLUTE. Briefly, I have deceived your aunt — I was in-formed that my new rival was to visit here this evening, and contriving to have him kept away, have passed myself on her for Captain Absolute.

LYDIA. O charming! And she really takes you for young Absolute!

ABSOLUTE. Oh, she's convinced of it.   160

LYDIA. Ha! ha! ha! I can't forbear laughing to think how her sagacity is overreached!

ABSOLUTE. But we trifle with our precious moments — such another opportunity may not occur; then let me now con-jure my kind, my condescending angel, to fix the time when I may rescue her from undeserving persecution, and with a licensed warmth plead for my reward.

LYDIA. Will you then, Beverley, consent to forfeit that por-tion of my paltry wealth? — that burden on the wings of love?   170

ABSOLUTE. Oh, come to me — rich only thus — in loveliness! Bring no portion to me but thy love — 'twill be generous in you, Lydia — for well you know, it is the only dower your poor Beverley can repay.

LYDIA. [*Aside*]. How persuasive are his words! — how charming will poverty be with him!

ABSOLUTE. Ah! my soul, what a life will we then live! Love shall be our idol and support! we will worship him with a monastic strictness; abjuring all worldly toys, to centre
180 every thought and action there. Proud of calamity, we will enjoy the wreck of wealth: while the surrounding gloom of adversity shall make the flame of our pure love show doubly bright. By Heavens! I would fling all goods of fortune from me with a prodigal hand, to enjoy the scene where I might clasp my Lydia to my bosom, and say, the world affords no smile to me but here — [*Embracing her.*] [*Aside*]. If she holds out now, the devil is in it!

LYDIA. [*Aside*]. Now could I fly with him to the antipodes! but my persecution is not yet come to a crisis.

Re-enter MRS. MALAPROP, *listening*

190 MRS. MALAPROP. [*Aside*]. I am impatient to know how the little hussy deports herself.

ABSOLUTE. So pensive, Lydia! — is then your warmth abated?

MRS. MALAPROP. [*Aside*]. Warmth abated! — so! — she has been in a passion, I suppose.

LYDIA. No — nor ever can while I have life.

MRS. MALAPROP. [*Aside*]. An ill-tempered little devil! She'll be in a passion all her life — will she?

LYDIA. Think not the idle threats of my ridiculous aunt can
200 ever have any weight with me.

MRS. MALAPROP. [*Aside*]. Very dutiful, upon my word!

---

l.188 antipodes: *other side of the world.*

LYDIA. Let her choice be Captain Absolute, but Beverley is mine.

MRS. MALAPROP. [*Aside*]. I am astonished at her assurance! — to his face — this is to his face!

ABSOLUTE. Thus then let me enforce my suit.   [*Kneeling.*

MRS. MALAPROP. [*Aside*]. Ay, poor young man! — down on his knees entreating for pity! — I can contain no longer. — [*Coming forward.*] Why, thou vixen! — I have overheard you.   210

ABSOLUTE. [*Aside*]. Oh, confound her vigilance!

MRS. MALAPROP. Captain Absolute, I know not how to apologize for her shocking rudeness.

ABSOLUTE. [*Aside*]. So all's safe, I find. — [*Aloud.*] I have hopes, madam, that time will bring the young lady ——

MRS. MALAPROP. Oh, there's nothing to be hoped for from her! she's as headstrong as an allegory on the banks of Nile.

LYDIA. Nay, madam, what do you charge me with now?

MRS. MALAPROP. Why, thou unblushing rebel — didn't you 220 tell this gentleman to his face that you loved another better? — didn't you say you never would be his?

LYDIA. No, madam — I did not.

MRS. MALAPROP. Good Heavens! what assurance! — Lydia, Lydia, you ought to know that lying don't become a young woman! — Didn't you boast that Beverley, that stroller Beverley, possessed your heart? — Tell me that, I say.

LYDIA. 'Tis true, ma'am, and none but Beverley ——

MRS. MALAPROP. Hold! — hold, Assurance! — you shall 230 not be so rude.

ABSOLUTE. Nay, pray, Mrs. Malaprop, don't stop the young lady's speech: she's very welcome to talk thus — it does not hurt me in the least, I assure you.

MRS. MALAPROP. You are too good, captain — too amiably patient — but come with me, miss. — Let us see you again soon, captain — remember what we have fixed.

ABSOLUTE. I shall, ma'am.

MRS. MALAPROP. Come, take a graceful leave of the gentle-240 man.

LYDIA. May every blessing wait on my Beverley, my loved Bev ——

MRS. MALAPROP. Hussy! I'll choke the word in your throat! — come along — come along.

[*Exeunt severally*; CAPTAIN ABSOLUTE *kissing his hand to* LYDIA — MRS. MALAPROP *stopping her from speaking*

SCENE IV *Acres' Lodgings*

ACRES, *as just dressed, and* DAVID

ACRES. Indeed, David — do you think I become it so?

DAVID. You are quite another creature, believe me, master, by the mass! an we've any luck we shall see the Devon monkerony in all the print-shops in Bath!

ACRES. Dress does make a difference, David.

DAVID. 'Tis all in all, I think. — Difference! why, an you were to go now to Clod-hall, I am certain the old lady wouldn't know you: master Butler wouldn't believe his own eyes, and Mrs. Pickle would cry, Lard presarve me!
10 Our dairy-maid would come giggling to the door, and I warrant Dolly Tester, your honour's favourite, would blush like my waistcoat. — Oons! I'll hold a gallon, there an't a dog in the house but would bark, and I question whether Phillis would wag a hair of her tail!

ACRES. Ay, David, there's nothing like polishing.

DAVID. So I says of your honour's boots; but the boy never heeds me!

---

l.4 monkerony: *David's mistake for macaroni, a dandy.*

ACRES. But, David, has Mr. De-la-grace been here? I must rub up my balancing, and chasing, and boring.

DAVID. I'll call again, sir.   20

ACRES. Do — and see if there are any letters for me at the post-office.

DAVID. I will. — By the mass, I can't help looking at your head! — if I hadn't been at the cooking, I wish I may die if I should have known the dish again myself!   [*Exit.*

ACRES. [*Practising a dancing-step*]. Sink, slide — coupee. — Confound the first inventors of cotillons! say I — they are as bad as algebra to us country gentlemen — I can walk a minuet easy enough when I am forced! — and I have been accounted a good stick in a country-dance. — Odds 30 jigs and tabors! I never valued your cross-over to couple — figure in — right and left — and I'd foot it with e'er a captain in the county! — but these outlandish heathen allemandes and cotillons are quite beyond me! — I shall never prosper at 'em, that's sure — mine are true-born English legs — they don't understand their curst French lingo! — their *pas* this, and *pas* that, and *pas* t'other! — my feet don't like to be called paws! no, 'tis certain I have most Antigallican toes!

Enter SERVANT

SERVANT. Here is Sir Lucius O'Trigger to wait on you, sir. 40

ACRES. Show him in.

[*Exit* SERVANT

---

l.18 Mr. De-la-grace: *evidently a dancing master.*
l.19 balancing, and chasing, and boring: *dancing terms*; balance: *advance-retire*; chase: *a quick step*; bore: *a slow step.*
l.26 coupee: *a dancing step.*
l.27 cotillon: *a dance.*
l.31 tabors: *small drums*; cross-over to couple: *dancing terms.*
l.34 allemande: *a German dance resembling the waltz.*
l.37 pas: *Fr. step.*
l.39 Antigallican: *anti-French.*

Enter SIR LUCIUS O'TRIGGER

SIR LUCIUS. Mr. Acres, I am delighted to embrace you.

ACRES. My dear Sir Lucius, I kiss your hands.

SIR LUCIUS. Pray, my friend, what has brought you so suddenly to Bath?

ACRES. Faith! I have followed Cupid's Jack-a-lantern, and find myself in a quagmire at last. — In short, I have been very ill-used, Sir Lucius. — I don't choose to mention names, but look on me as on a very ill-used gentleman.

50 SIR LUCIUS. Pray what is the case? — I ask no names.

ACRES. Mark me, Sir Lucius, I fall as deep as need be in love with a young lady — her friends take my part — I follow her to Bath — send word of my arrival; and receive answer, that the lady is to be otherwise disposed of. — This, Sir Lucius, I call being ill-used.

SIR LUCIUS. Very ill, upon my conscience. — Pray, can you divine the cause of it?

ACRES. Why, there's the matter; she has another lover, one Beverley, who, I am told, is now in Bath. — Odds slanders
60 and lies! he must be at the bottom of it.

SIR LUCIUS. A rival in the case, is there? — and you think he has supplanted you unfairly?

ACRES. Unfairly! to be sure he has. He never could have done it fairly.

SIR LUCIUS. Then sure you know what is to be done!

ACRES. Not I, upon my soul!

SIR LUCIUS. We wear no swords here, but you understand me.

ACRES. What! fight him!

70 SIR LUCIUS. Ay, to be sure: what can I mean else?

ACRES. But he has given me no provocation.

---

l.46 Jack-a-lantern: *will-o'-the-wisp.*

SIR LUCIUS. Now, I think he has given you the greatest
provocation in the world. Can a man commit a more
heinous offence against another than to fall in love with
the same woman? Oh, by my soul! it is the most unpardon-
able breach of friendship.

ACRES. Breach of friendship! ay, ay; but I have no acquaintance with this man. I never saw him in my life.

SIR LUCIUS. That's no argument at all — he has the less
right then to take such a liberty.   80

ACRES. Gad, that's true — I grow full of anger, Sir Lucius!
— I fire apace! Odds hilts and blades! I find a man may
have a deal of valour in him, and not know it! But
couldn't I contrive to have a little right of my side?

SIR LUCIUS. What the devil signifies right, when your
honour is concerned? Do you think Achilles, or my little
Alexander the Great, ever inquired where the right lay?
No, by my soul, they drew their broadswords, and left the
lazy sons of peace to settle the justice of it.

ACRES. Your words are a grenadier's march to my heart! I 90
believe courage must be catching! I certainly do feel a
kind of valour rising as it were — a kind of courage, as I
may say. — Odds flints, pans, and triggers! I'll challenge
him directly.

SIR LUCIUS. Ah, my little friend, if I had Blunderbuss Hall
here, I could show you a range of ancestry, in the O'Trigger line, that would furnish the new room; every one of
whom had killed his man! — For though the mansion-
house and dirty acres have slipped through my fingers, I

---

l.86 Achilles: *the Greek hero of Homer's* Iliad.
l.87 Alexander the Great: *the famous Greek conqueror of the then
known world* (356-323 B.C.).
l.88 broadsword: *a sword with a broad blade and a sharp edge.*
l.90 are a grenadier's march to my heart: *inspire me with courage
as the sound of grenadiers on the march would do.*
l.93 flints: *used to ignite the powder in guns*; pans: *the part of the
gun which held the powder.*

100   thank heaven our honour and the family pictures are as fresh as ever.

ACRES. O, Sir Lucius! I have had ancestors too! — every man of 'em colonel or captain in the militia! — Odds balls and barrels! say no more — I'm braced for it. The thunder of your words has soured the milk of human kindness in my breast; — Zounds! as the man in the play says, *I could do such deeds!*

SIR LUCIUS. Come, come, there must be no passion at all in the case — these things should always be done civilly.

110   ACRES. I must be in a passion, Sir Lucius — I must be in a rage. — Dear Sir Lucius, let me be in a rage, if you love me. Come, here's pen and paper. — [*Sits down to write.*] I would the ink were red! — Indite, I say indite! — How shall I begin? Odds bullets and blades! I'll write a good bold hand, however.

SIR LUCIUS. Pray compose yourself.

ACRES. Come — now, shall I begin with an oath? Do, Sir Lucius, let me begin with a damme.

SIR LUCIUS. Pho! pho! do the thing decently, and like a
120   Christian. Begin now — *Sir* ——

ACRES. That's too civil by half.

SIR LUCIUS. *To prevent the confusion that might arise* ——

ACRES. Well —

SIR LUCIUS. *From our both addressing the same lady* ——

ACRES. Ay, there's the reason — *same lady* — well ——

SIR LUCIUS. *I shall expect the honour of your company* ——

ACRES. Zounds! I'm not asking him to dinner.

SIR LUCIUS. Pray be easy.

---

ll.103-4 balls and barrels: *the reference is still to firearms.*
ll.105-6 the milk of human kindness: *see* Macbeth, *I. v.* 15, 16.
ll.106-7 as the man in the play says, 'I could do such deeds!': *see* Hamlet, *III. ii.* 408.

ACRES. Well then, *honour of your company* ——

SIR LUCIUS. *To settle our pretensions* ——   130

ACRES. Well.

SIR LUCIUS. Let me see, ay, King's-Mead-Fields will do —
in King's-Mead-Fields.

ACRES. So, that's done — Well, I'll fold it up presently; my
own crest — a hand and dagger shall be the seal.

SIR LUCIUS. You see now this little explanation will put a
stop at once to all confusion or misunderstanding that
might arise between you.

ACRES. Ay, we fight to prevent any misunderstanding.

SIR LUCIUS. Now, I'll leave you to fix your own time. Take 140
my advice, and you'll decide it this evening if you can;
then let the worst come of it, 'twill be off your mind to-
morrow.

ACRES. Very true.

SIR LUCIUS. So I shall see nothing more of you, unless it be
by letter, till the evening. — I would do myself the honour
to carry your message; but, to tell you a secret, I believe I
shall have just such another affair on my own hands.
There is a gay captain here, who put a jest on me lately, at
the expense of my country, and I only want to fall in 150
with the gentleman, to call him out.

ACRES. By my valour, I should like to see you fight first!
Odds life! I should like to see you kill him if it was only to
get a little lesson.

SIR LUCIUS. I shall be very proud of instructing you. —
Well, for the present — but remember now, when you
meet your antagonist, do everything in a mild and agreeable manner. — Let your courage be as keen, but at the
same time as polished, as your sword.   [*Exeunt severally.*

---

l.132 King's-Mead-Fields: *on the south-west of Bath.*

ACT IV

SCENE I. *Acres' Lodgings*

ACRES *and* DAVID

DAVID. Then, by the mass, sir! I would do no such thing —
ne'er a Sir Lucius O'Trigger in the kingdom should make
me fight, when I wa'n't so minded. Oons! what will the
old lady say when she hears o't?

ACRES. Ah! David, if you had heard Sir Lucius! — Odds
sparks and flames! he would have roused your valour.

DAVID. Not he, indeed. I hate such bloodthirsty cormorants.
Look'ee, master, if you'd wanted a bout at boxing,
quarter-staff, or short-staff, I should never be the man to
10 bid you cry off: but for your curst sharps and snaps, I
never knew any good come of 'em.

ACRES. But my honour, David, my honour! I must be very
careful of my honour.

DAVID. Ay, by the mass! and I would be very careful of it;
and I think in return my honour couldn't do less than to
be very careful of me.

ACRES. Odds blades! David, no gentleman will ever risk the
loss of his honour.

DAVID. I say then, it would be but civil in honour never to
20 risk the loss of a gentleman. — Look'ee, master, this
honour seems to me to be a marvellous false friend: ay,
truly, a very courtier-like servant. — Put the case, I was a
gentleman (which, thank God, no one can say of me:)
well — my honour makes me quarrel with another gentleman of my acquaintance. — So — we fight. (Pleasant
enough that!) Boh! I kill him — (the more's my luck!)

---

l.7 cormorant: *a sea bird, an emblem of ferocious greed.*
l.9 quarter-staff, or short-staff: *methods of fighting with staves.*
l.10 sharps and snaps: *sharpers and cheats.*
ll.20-1 this honour, etc.: *the observations of David and Acres on
honour echo Falstaff's soliloquy. See* I Henry IV, *V. i.* 129-40.

now, pray who gets the profit of it? — Why, my honour.
But put the case that he kills me! — by the mass! I go to
the worms, and my honour whips over to my enemy.

ACRES. No, David — in that case — Odds crowns and 30
laurels! — your honour follows you to the grave.

DAVID. Now, that's just the place where I could make a
shift to do without it.

ACRES. Zounds! David, you are a coward! — It doesn't
become my valour to listen to you. — What, shall I disgrace my ancestors? — Think of that, David — think what
it would be to disgrace my ancestors.

DAVID. Under favour, the surest way of not disgracing them,
is to keep as long as you can out of their company. Look'ee
now, master, to go to them in such haste — with an ounce 40
of lead in your brains — I should think might as well be
let alone. Our ancestors are very good kind of folks; but
they are the last people I should choose to have a visiting
acquaintance with.

ACRES. But, David, now, you don't think there is such very,
very, very great danger, hey? — Odds life! people often
fight without any mischief done!

DAVID. By the mass, I think 'tis ten to one against you! —
Oons! here to meet some lion-headed fellow, I warrant,
with his double-barrelled swords, and cut-and-thrust 50
pistols! — Lord bless us! it makes me tremble to think
o't — Those be such desperate bloody-minded weapons!
Well, I never could abide 'em — from a child I never
could fancy 'em! — I suppose there an't been so merciless
a beast in the world as your loaded pistol!

ACRES. Zounds! I won't be afraid! — Odds fire and fury!
you shan't make me afraid. — Here is the challenge, and I
have sent for my dear friend Jack Absolute to carry it for
me.

DAVID. Ay, i' the name of mischief, let him be the mes- 60
senger. — For my part, I wouldn't lend a hand to it for the
best horse in your stable. By the mass! it don't look like

another letter. It is, as I may say, a designing and mali-
cious-looking letter; and I warrant smells of gunpowder
like a soldier's pouch! — Oons! I wouldn't swear it
mayn't go off!

ACRES. Out, you poltroon! you ha'n't the valour of a grass-
hopper.

DAVID. Well, I say no more — 'twill be sad news, to be sure,
70   at Clod-Hall! but I ha' done. — How Phillis will howl
when she hears of it! — Ay, poor bitch, she little thinks
what shooting her master's going after! And I warrant old
Crop, who has carried your honour, field and road, these
ten years, will curse the hour he was born. [*Whimpering.*

ACRES. It won't do, David — I am determined to fight — so
get along, you coward, while I'm in the mind.

Enter SERVANT

SERVANT. Captain Absolute, sir.

ACRES. Oh! show him up.   [*Exit* SERVANT.

DAVID. Well, Heaven send we be all alive this time to-
80   morrow.

ACRES. What's that? — Don't provoke me, David!

DAVID. Good-bye, master.   [*Whimpering.*

ACRES. Get along, you cowardly, dastardly, croaking raven!
[*Exit* DAVID.

Enter CAPTAIN ABSOLUTE

ABSOLUTE. What's the matter, Bob?

ACRES. A vile, sheep-hearted blockhead! If I hadn't the
valour of St. George and the dragon to boot —

ABSOLUTE. But what did you want with me, Bob?

ACRES. Oh! — There —   [*Gives him the challenge.*

ABSOLUTE. [*Aside*]. *To Ensign Beverley*. — So, what's going
90   on now! — [*Aloud.*] Well, what's this?

---

l.67 poltroon: *a coward.*
l.86 to boot: *in addition.*

ACRES. A challenge!

ABSOLUTE. Indeed! Why, you won't fight him; will you, Bob?

ACRES. Egad, but I will, Jack. Sir Lucius has wrought me to it. He has left me full of rage — and I'll fight this evening, that so much good passion mayn't be wasted.

ABSOLUTE. But what have I to do with this?

ACRES. Why, as I think you know something of this fellow, I want you to find him out for me, and give him this mortal defiance.   100

ABSOLUTE. Well, give it to me, and trust me he gets it.

ACRES. Thank you, my dear friend, my dear Jack; but it is giving you a great deal of trouble.

ABSOLUTE. Not in the least — I beg you won't mention it. — No trouble in the world, I assure you.

ACRES. You are very kind. — What it is to have a friend! — You couldn't be my second, could you, Jack?

ABSOLUTE. Why no, Bob — not in this affair — it would not be quite so proper.

ACRES. Well, then, I must get my friend Sir Lucius. I shall   110 have your good wishes, however, Jack?

ABSOLUTE. Whenever he meets you, believe me.

Re-enter SERVANT

SERVANT. Sir Anthony Absolute is below, inquiring for the captain.

ABSOLUTE. I'll come instantly. — [*Exit* SERVANT.] Well, my little hero, success attend you.   [*Going.*

ACRES. Stay — stay, Jack. — If Beverley should ask you what kind of a man your friend Acres is, do tell him I am a devil of a fellow — will you, Jack?

ABSOLUTE. To be sure I shall. I'll say you are a determined   120 dog — hey, Bob?

ACRES. Ay, do, do — and if that frightens him, egad, perhaps he mayn't come. So tell him I generally kill a man a week; will you, Jack?

ABSOLUTE. I will, I will; I'll say you are called in the country Fighting Bob.

ACRES. Right — right — 'tis all to prevent mischief; for I don't want to take his life if I clear my honour.

ABSOLUTE. No! — that's very kind of you.

130 ACRES. Why, you don't wish me to kill him — do you, Jack?

ABSOLUTE. No, upon my soul, I do not. But a devil of a fellow, hey? [Going.

ACRES. True, true — but stay — stay, Jack — you may add, that you never saw me in such a rage before — a most devouring rage!

ABSOLUTE. I will, I will.

ACRES. Remember, Jack — a determined dog.

ABSOLUTE. Ay, ay, Fighting Bob! [Exeunt severally.

SCENE II. *Mrs. Malaprop's Lodgings*

MRS. MALAPROP *and* LYDIA

MRS. MALAPROP. Why, thou perverse one! — tell me what you can object to him? Isn't he a handsome man? — tell me that. A genteel man? a pretty figure of a man?

LYDIA. [*Aside*]. She little thinks whom she is praising! — [*Aloud.*] So is Beverley, ma'am.

MRS. MALAPROP. No caparisons, miss, if you please. Caparisons don't become a young woman. No! Captain Absolute is indeed a fine gentleman!

LYDIA. [*Aside*]. Ay, the Captain Absolute you have seen.

10 MRS. MALAPROP. Then he's so well bred; — so full of alacrity, and adulation! — and has so much to say for himself: — in such good language too! His physiognomy

so grammatical! Then his presence is so noble! I protest,
when I saw him, I thought of what Hamlet says in the
play:—

> 'Hesperian curls — the front of Job himself! —
> An eye, like March, to threaten at command! —
> A station, like Harry Mercury, new ——'

Something about kissing — on a hill — however, the simi-
litude struck me directly.   20

LYDIA. [*Aside*]. How enraged she'll be presently, when she
discovers her mistake!

Enter SERVANT

SERVANT. Sir Anthony and Captain Absolute are below,
ma'am.

MRS. MALAPROP. Show them up here. —   [*Exit* SERVANT.]
Now, Lydia, I insist on your behaving as becomes a
young woman. Show your good breeding, at least, though
you have forgot your duty.

LYDIA. Madam, I have told you my resolution! — I shall
not only give him no encouragement, but I won't even 30
speak to, or look at him.

[*Flings herself into a chair, with her face from the door.*

Enter SIR ANTHONY ABSOLUTE *and* CAPTAIN ABSOLUTE

SIR ANTHONY. Here we are, Mrs. Malaprop; come to miti-
gate the frowns of unrelenting beauty, — and difficulty
enough I had to bring this fellow. — I don't know what's
the matter; but if I had not held him by force, he'd have
given me the slip.

MRS. MALAPROP. You have infinite trouble, Sir Anthony,
in the affair. I am ashamed for the cause! — [*Aside to*
LYDIA.] Lydia, Lydia, rise, I beseech you! — pay your
respects!   40

---

ll.15-17 'Hesperian curls,' etc.: *for the correct words see* Hamlet,
III. iv. 56-59.

SIR ANTHONY. I hope, madam, that Miss Languish has reflected on the worth of this gentleman, and the regard due to her aunt's choice, and my alliance. — [*Aside to* CAPTAIN ABSOLUTE.] Now, Jack, speak to her.

ABSOLUTE. [*Aside*]. What the devil shall I do! — [*Aside to* SIR ANTHONY.] You see, sir, she won't even look at me whilst you are here. I knew she wouldn't! I told you so. Let me entreat you, sir, to leave us together!

[*Seems to expostulate with his father.*

LYDIA. [*Aside*]. I wonder I ha'n't heard my aunt exclaim
50 yet! sure she can't have looked at him! — perhaps their regimentals are alike, and she is something blind.

SIR ANTHONY. I say, sir, I won't stir a foot yet!

MRS. MALAPROP. I am sorry to say, Sir Anthony, that my affluence over my niece is very small. — [*Aside to* LYDIA.] Turn round, Lydia: I blush for you!

SIR ANTHONY. May I not flatter myself, that Miss Languish will assign what cause of dislike she can have to my son! — [*Aside to* CAPTAIN ABSOLUTE.] Why don't you begin, Jack? — Speak, you puppy — speak!

60 MRS. MALAPROP. It is impossible, Sir Anthony, she can have any. She will not say she has. — [*Aside to* LYDIA.] Answer, hussy! why don't you answer?

SIR ANTHONY. Then, madam, I trust that a childish and hasty predilection will be no bar to Jack's happiness. — [*Aside to* CAPTAIN ABSOLUTE.] — Zounds! sirrah! why don't you speak?

LYDIA. [*Aside*]. I think my lover seems as little inclined to conversation as myself. — How strangely blind my aunt must be!

70 ABSOLUTE. Hem! hem! madam — hem! — [*Attempts to speak, then returns to* SIR ANTHONY.] Faith! sir, I am so confounded! — and — so — so — confused! — I told you I should be so, sir — I knew it. — The — the — tremor of my passion entirely takes away my presence of mind.

SIR ANTHONY. But it don't take away your voice, fool, does it? — Go up, and speak to her directly!

[CAPTAIN ABSOLUTE *makes signs to* MRS. MALAPROP *to leave them together.*

MRS. MALAPROP. Sir Anthony, shall we leave them together? — [*Aside to* LYDIA.] Ah! you stubborn little vixen!

SIR ANTHONY. Not yet, ma'am, not yet! — [*Aside to* 80 CAPTAIN ABSOLUTE.] What the devil are you at? unlock your jaws, sirrah, or ——

ABSOLUTE. [*Aside*]. Now Heaven send she may be too sullen to look round! — I must disguise my voice. — [*Draws near* LYDIA, *and speaks in a low hoarse tone.*] Will not Miss Languish lend an ear to the mild accents of true love? Will not ——

SIR ANTHONY. What the devil ails the fellow? Why don't you speak out? — not stand croaking like a frog in a quinsy!   90

ABSOLUTE. The — the — excess of my awe, and my — my — my modesty, quite choke me!

SIR ANTHONY. Ah! your modesty again! — I'll tell you what, Jack; if you don't speak out directly, and glibly too, I shall be in such a rage! — Mrs. Malaprop, I wish the lady would favour us with something more than a side-front.   [MRS. MALAPROP *seems to chide* LYDIA.

ABSOLUTE. [*Aside*]. So all will out, I see! — [*Goes up to* LYDIA, *speaks softly.*] Be not surprised, my Lydia, suppress all surprise at present.   100

LYDIA. [*Aside*]. Heavens! 'tis Beverley's voice! Sure he can't have imposed on Sir Anthony too! — [*Looks round by degrees, then starts up.*] Is this possible! — my Beverley! — how can this be? — my Beverley?

ABSOLUTE. [*Aside*]. Ah! 'tis all over.

---

ll.89-90 a quinsy: *an inflammation of the throat.*

SIR ANTHONY. Beverley! — the devil — Beverley! — What can the girl mean? — This is my son, Jack Absolute.

MRS. MALAPROP. For shame, hussy! for shame! your head runs so on that fellow, that you have him always in your
110 eyes! — beg Captain Absolute's pardon directly.

LYDIA. I see no Captain Absolute, but my loved Beverley!

SIR ANTHONY. Zounds! the girl's mad! — her brain's turned by reading.

MRS. MALAPROP. O' my conscience, I believe so! — What do you mean by Beverley, hussy? — You saw Captain Absolute before to-day; there he is — your husband that shall be.

LYDIA. With all my soul, ma'am — when I refuse my Beverley ——

120 SIR ANTHONY. Oh! she's as mad as Bedlam! — or has this fellow been playing us a rogue's trick! — Come here, sirrah; who the devil are you?

ABSOLUTE. Faith, sir, I am not quite clear myself; but I'll endeavour to recollect.

SIR ANTHONY. Are you my son or not? — answer for your mother, you dog, if you won't for me.

MRS. MALAPROP. Ay, sir, who are you? O mercy! I begin to suspect! —

ABSOLUTE. [Aside]. Ye powers of impudence, befriend me!
130 — [Aloud.] Sir Anthony, most assuredly I am your wife's son and that I sincerely believe myself to be yours also, I hope my duty has always shown. — Mrs. Malaprop, I am your most respectful admirer, and shall be proud to add affectionate nephew. — I need not tell my Lydia, that she sees her faithful Beverley, who, knowing the singular generosity of her temper, assumed that name and station, which has proved a test of the most disinterested love, which he now hopes to enjoy in a more elevated character.

---

l.120 Bedlam: *the first London lunatic asylum.*

LYDIA. [*Sullenly*]. So! — there will be no elopement after all! 140

SIR ANTHONY. Upon my soul, Jack, thou art a very impudent fellow! to do you justice, I think I never saw a piece of more consummate assurance!

ABSOLUTE. Oh, you flatter me, sir — you compliment — 'tis my modesty you know, sir, — my modesty that has stood in my way.

SIR ANTHONY. Well, I am glad you are not the dull, insensible· varlet you pretended to be, however! — I'm glad you have made a fool of your father, you dog — I am. So this was your *penitence*, your *duty* and *obedience!* — I 150 thought it was sudden! — *You never heard their names before*, not you! — *what, the Languishes of Worcestershire*, hey? — *if you could please me in the affair it was all you desired!* — Ah! you dissembling villain! — What! — [*Pointing to* LYDIA] *she squints, don't she? — a little red-haired girl!* — hey? — Why, you hypocritical young rascal! — I wonder you a'n't ashamed to hold up your head!

ABSOLUTE. 'Tis with difficulty, sir. — I am confused — very much confused, as you must perceive.

MRS. MALAPROP. O Lud! Sir Anthony! — a new light 160 breaks in upon me! — hey! — how! what! captain, did you write the letters then? — What — am I to thank you for the elegant compilation of *an old weather-beaten she-dragon* — hey! — O mercy! — was it you that reflected on my parts of speech?

ABSOLUTE. Dear sir! my modesty will be overpowered at last, if you don't assist me — I shall certainly not be able to stand it!

SIR ANTHONY. Come, come, Mrs. Malaprop, we must forget and forgive; — odds life! matters have taken so clever 170 a turn all of a sudden, that I could find in my heart to be so good-humoured! and so gallant! hey! Mrs. Malaprop!

---

ll.142-3 a piece ... assurance: *as we might say 'anything so cool'.*

MRS. MALAPROP. Well, Sir Anthony, since you desire it, we will not anticipate the past! — so mind, young people — our retrospection will be all to the future.

SIR ANTHONY. Come, we must leave them together; Mrs. Malaprop, they long to fly into each other's arms, I warrant! — Jack — isn't the cheek as I said, hey? — and the eye, you rogue! — and the lip — hey? Come, Mrs. Mala-
180 prop, we'll not disturb their tenderness — theirs is the time of life for happiness! — *Youth's the season made for joy* — [*Sings.*] — hey! — Odds life! I'm in such spirits, — I don't know what I could not do! — Permit me, ma'am — [*Gives his hand to* MRS. MALAPROP.] Tol-de-rol — 'gad, I should like to have a little fooling myself — Tol-de-rol! de-rol.

[*Exit, singing and handing* MRS. MALAPROP. — LYDIA *sits sullenly in her chair.*

ABSOLUTE. [*Aside*]. So much thought bodes me no good. — [*Aloud.*] So grave, Lydia!

LYDIA. Sir!

ABSOLUTE. [*Aside*]. So! — egad! I thought as much! — that
190 monosyllable has froze me! — [*Aloud.*] What, Lydia, now that we are as happy in our friends' consent, as in our mutual vows ——

LYDIA. [*Peevishly*]. Friends' consent indeed!

ABSOLUTE. Come, come, we must lay aside some of our romance — a little wealth and comfort may be endured after all. And for your fortune, the lawyers shall make such settlements as ——

LYDIA. Lawyers! I hate lawyers!

ABSOLUTE. Nay, then, we will not wait for their lingering
200 forms, but instantly procure the licence, and ——

LYDIA. The licence! — I hate licence!

ABSOLUTE. [*Kneeling*]. Oh, my love! be not so unkind! — thus let me entreat —

---

l.181 'Youth's the season made for joy': *a quotation from Gay's* Beggar's Opera (1727).

LYDIA. Pshaw! — what signifies kneeling, when you know I must have you?

ABSOLUTE. [*Rising*]. Nay, madam, there shall be no constraint upon your inclinations, I promise you. — If I have lost your heart, I resign the rest — [*Aside.*] 'Gad, I must try what a little spirit will do.

LYDIA. [*Rising*]. Then, sir, let me tell you, the interest you 210 had there was acquired by a mean, unmanly imposition, and deserved the punishment of fraud. — What, you have been treating me like a child! — humouring my romance! and laughing, I suppose, at your success!

ABSOLUTE. You wrong me, Lydia, you wrong me — only hear ——

LYDIA. So, while I fondly imagined we were deceiving my relations, and flattered myself that I should outwit and incense them all — behold my hopes are to be crushed at once, by my aunt's consent and approbation — and I am 220 myself the only dupe at last! — [*Walking about in a heat.*] But here, sir, here is the picture — Beverley's picture! [*taking a miniature from her bosom*] which I have worn, night and day, in spite of threats and entreaties! — There, sir; [*flings it to him*] and be assured I throw the original from my heart as easily.

ABSOLUTE. Nay, nay, ma'am, we will not differ as to that. — Here, [*taking out a picture*] here is Miss Lydia Languish. — What a difference! — ay, there is the heavenly assenting smile that first gave soul and spirit to my hopes! 230 — those are the lips which sealed a vow, as yet scarce dry in Cupid's calendar! and there the half-resentful blush, that would have checked the ardour of my thanks! — Well, all that's past! — all over indeed! — There, madam — in beauty, that copy is not equal to you, but in my mind its merit over the original, in being still the same, is such — that — I cannot find in my heart to part with it.

[*Puts it up again.*

LYDIA. [*Softening*]. 'Tis your own doing, sir — I — I — I suppose you are perfectly satisfied.

240 ABSOLUTE. O, most certainly — sure, now, this is much better than being in love! — ha! ha! ha! — there's some spirit in this! — What signifies breaking some scores of solemn promises:—all that's of no consequence, you know.—To be sure people will say, that miss don't know her own mind — but never mind that! Or, perhaps, they may be ill-natured enough to hint, that the gentleman grew tired of the lady and forsook her — but don't let that fret you.

LYDIA. There is no bearing his insolence.

[*Bursts into tears.*

Re-enter MRS. MALAPROP *and* SIR ANTHONY ABSOLUTE

250 MRS. MALAPROP. Come, we must interrupt your billing and cooing awhile.

LYDIA. [*Sobbing*]. This is worse than your treachery and deceit, you base ingrate!

SIR ANTHONY. What the devil's the matter now! — Zounds! Mrs. Malaprop, this is the oddest billing and cooing I ever heard! — but what the deuce is the meaning of it? — I am quite astonished!

ABSOLUTE. Ask the lady, sir.

MRS. MALAPROP. O mercy! — I'm quite analysed, for my
260 part! — Why, Lydia, what is the reason of this?

LYDIA. Ask the gentleman, ma'am.

SIR ANTHONY. Zounds! I shall be in a frenzy! — Why, Jack, you are not come out to be any one else, are you?

MRS. MALAPROP. Ay, sir, there's no more trick, is there? — you are not like Cerberus, three gentlemen at once, are you?

1.265 like Cerberus, three gentlemen at once: *Cerberus was the three-headed dog in classical mythology who guarded the entrance to the lower world.*

ABSOLUTE. You'll not let me speak — I say the lady can account for this much better than I can.

LYDIA. Ma'am, you once commanded me never to think of Beverley again — there is the man — I now obey you: for, from this moment, I renounce him for ever.   [*Exit.*

MRS. MALAPROP. O mercy! and miracles! what a turn here is — why sure, captain, you haven't behaved disrespectfully to my niece.

SIR ANTHONY. Ha! ha! ha! — ha! ha! ha! — now I see it. Ha! ha! ha! — now I see it — you have been too lively, Jack.

ABSOLUTE. Nay, sir, upon my word ——

SIR ANTHONY. Come, no lying, Jack — I'm sure 'twas so.

MRS. MALAPROP. O Lud! Sir Anthony! — O fie, captain!

ABSOLUTE. Upon my soul, ma'am ——

SIR ANTHONY. Come, no excuses, Jack; why, your father, you rogue, was so before you: — the blood of the Absolutes was always impatient. — Ha! ha! ha! poor little Lydia! why, you've frightened her, you dog, you have.

ABSOLUTE. By all that's good, sir ——

SIR ANTHONY. Zounds! say no more, I tell you — Mrs. Malaprop shall make your peace. — You must make his peace, Mrs. Malaprop:—you must tell her 'tis Jack's way — tell her 'tis all our ways — it runs in the blood of our family! — Come away, Jack — Ha! ha! ha! Mrs. Malaprop — a young villain!   [*Pushing him out.*

MRS. MALAPROP. O! Sir Anthony! — O fie, captain!
[*Exeunt severally.*

SCENE III. *The North Parade*

Enter SIR LUCIUS O'TRIGGER

SIR LUCIUS. I wonder where this Captain Absolute hides himself! Upon my conscience! these officers are always in one's way in love affairs: — I remember I might have married Lady Dorothy Carmine, if it had not been for a little rogue of a major, who ran away with her before she could get a sight of me! And I wonder too what it is the ladies can see in them to be so fond of them — unless it be a touch of the old serpent in 'em, that makes the little creatures be caught, like vipers, with a bit of red cloth. Ha!
10 isn't this the captain coming? — faith it is! — There is a probability of succeeding about that fellow, that is mighty provoking! Who is he talking to?   [*Steps aside.*

Enter CAPTAIN ABSOLUTE

ABSOLUTE. [*Aside*]. To what fine purpose I have been plotting! a noble reward for all my schemes, upon my soul! — a little gipsy! — I did not think her romance could have made her so absurd either. 'Sdeath, I never was in a worse humour in my life! — I could cut my own throat, or any other person's, with the greatest pleasure in the world!

SIR LUCIUS. Oh, faith! I'm in the luck of it. I never could
20 have found him in a sweeter temper for my purpose — to be sure I'm just come in the nick! Now to enter into conversation with him, and so quarrel genteelly. — [*Goes up to* CAPTAIN ABSOLUTE.] With regard to that matter, captain, I must beg leave to differ in opinion with you.

ABSOLUTE. Upon my word, then, you must be a very subtle disputant: — because, sir, I happened just then to be giving no opinion at all.

SIR LUCIUS. That's no reason. For give me leave to tell you, a man may think an untruth as well as speak one.

---

l.21 nick: *the nick of time.*

ABSOLUTE. Very true, sir; but if a man never utters his thoughts, I should think they might stand a chance of escaping controversy.

SIR LUCIUS. Then, sir, you differ in opinion with me, which amounts to the same thing.

ABSOLUTE. Hark'ee, Sir Lucius; if I had not before known you to be a gentleman, upon my soul, I should not have discovered it at this interview: for what you can drive at, unless you mean to quarrel with me, I cannot conceive!

SIR LUCIUS. I humbly thank you, sir, for the quickness of your apprehension. — [Bowing.] You have named the very thing I would be at.

ABSOLUTE. Very well, sir; I shall certainly not baulk your inclinations. — But I should be glad you would please to explain your motives.

SIR LUCIUS. Pray, sir, be easy; the quarrel is a very pretty quarrel as it stands; we should only spoil it by trying to explain it. However, your memory is very short, or you could not have forgot an affront you passed on me within this week. So, no more, but name your time and place.

ABSOLUTE. Well, sir, since you are so bent on it, the sooner the better; let it be this evening — here, by the Spring Gardens. We shall scarcely be interrupted.

SIR LUCIUS. Faith! that same interruption in affairs of this nature shows very great ill-breeding. I don't know what's the reason, but in England, if a thing of this kind gets wind, people make such a pother, that a gentleman can never fight in peace and quietness. However, if it's the same to you, captain, I should take it as a particular kindness if you'd let us meet in King's-Mead-Fields, as a little business will call me there about six o'clock, and I may despatch both matters at once.

ABSOLUTE. 'Tis the same to me exactly. A little after six, then, we will discuss this matter more seriously.

---

ll.51-2 the Spring Gardens: *well-known public gardens in Bath.*

SIR LUCIUS. If you please, sir; there will be very pretty
small-sword light, though it won't do for a long shot. So
that matter's settled, and my mind's at ease!   [*Exit.*

Enter FAULKLAND

ABSOLUTE. Well met! I was going to look for you. O Faulkland! all the demons of spite and disappointment have
conspired against me! I'm so vexed, that if I had not the
70   prospect of a resource in being knocked o' the head by-
and-by, I should scarce have spirits to tell you the cause.

FAULKLAND. What can you mean? — Has Lydia changed her
mind? — I should have thought her duty and inclination
would now have pointed to the same object.

ABSOLUTE. Ay, just as the eyes do of a person who squints:
when her love-eye was fixed on me, t'other, her eye of
duty, was finely obliqued: but when duty bid her point
that the same way, off t'other turned on a swivel, and
secured its retreat with a frown!

80 FAULKLAND. But what's the resource you ——

ABSOLUTE. Oh, to wind up the whole, a good-natured Irish-
man here has — [*Mimicking* SIR LUCIUS] — begged leave
to have the pleasure of cutting my throat; and I mean to
indulge him — that's all.

FAULKLAND. Prithee, be serious!

ABSOLUTE. 'Tis fact, upon my soul! Sir Lucius O'Trigger —
you know him by sight — for some affront, which I am
sure I never intended, has obliged me to meet him this
evening at six o'clock: 'tis on that account I wished to see
90   you; you must go with me.

FAULKLAND. Nay, there must be some mistake, sure. Sir
Lucius shall explain himself, and I dare say matters may
be accommodated. But this evening did you say? I wish it
had been any other time.

1.65 small-sword: *a light sword for fencing.*

ABSOLUTE. Why? there will be a light enough: there will (as Sir Lucius says) be very pretty small-sword light, though it will not do for a long shot. Confound his long shots!

FAULKLAND. But I am myself a good deal ruffled by a difference I have had with Julia. My vile tormenting temper has made me treat her so cruelly, that I shall not be myself 100 till we are reconciled.

ABSOLUTE. By Heavens! Faulkland, you don't deserve her!

Enter SERVANT, *gives* FAULKLAND *a letter, and exit*

FAULKLAND. Oh, Jack! this is from Julia. I dread to open it! I fear it may be to take a last leave! — perhaps to bid me return her letters, and restore —— Oh, how I suffer for my folly!

ABSOLUTE. Here, let me see. — [*Takes the letter and opens it.*] Ay, a final sentence, indeed! — 'tis all over with you, faith!

FAULKLAND. Nay, Jack, don't keep me in suspense!   110

ABSOLUTE. Hear then. — [*Reads*] *As I am convinced that my dear Faulkland's own reflections have already upbraided him for his last unkindness to me, I will not add a word on the subject. I wish to speak with you as soon as possible. Yours ever and truly,* JULIA. There's stubborness and resentment for you! — [*Gives him the letter.*] Why, man, you don't seem one whit the happier at this!

FAULKLAND. O yes, I am; but — but ——

ABSOLUTE. Confound your buts! you never hear anything that would make another man bless himself, but you 120 immediately damn it with a but!

FAULKLAND. Now, Jack, as you are my friend, own honestly — don't you think there is something forward, something indelicate, in this haste to forgive? Women should never sue for reconciliation: that should always come from us. They should retain their coldness till wooed to kindness; and their pardon, like their love, should 'not unsought be won'.

ABSOLUTE. I have not patience to listen to you! thou'rt
130   incorrigible! to say no more on the subject. I must go to
settle a few matters. Let me see you before six, remember,
at my lodgings. A poor industrious devil like me, who
have toiled, and drudged, and plotted to gain my ends,
and am at last disappointed by other people's folly, may
in pity be allowed to swear and grumble a little; but a
captious sceptic in love, a slave to fretfulness and whim,
who has no difficulties but of his own creating, is a subject
more fit for ridicule than compassion!   [*Exit.*

FAULKLAND. I feel his reproaches; yet I would not change
140   this too exquisite nicety for the gross content with which
he tramples on the thorns of love! His engaging me in this
duel has started an idea in my head, which I will instantly
pursue. I'll use it as the touchstone of Julia's sincerity and
disinterestedness. If her love prove pure and sterling ore,
my name will rest on it with honour; and once I've
stamped it there, I lay aside my doubts for ever! But if the
dross of selfishness, the alloy of pride, predominate,
'twill be best to leave her as a toy for some less cautious
fool to sigh for!   [*Exit.*

ACT V

SCENE I. *Julia's Dressing-room*

JULIA *discovered alone*

JULIA. How this message has alarmed me! what dreadful
accident can he mean? why such charge to be alone? — O
Faulkland! — how many unhappy moments — how many
tears have you cost me.

Enter FAULKLAND

JULIA. What means this? — why this caution, Faulkland?

FAULKLAND. Alas! Julia, I am come to take a long fare-
well.

JULIA. Heavens! what do you mean?

FAULKLAND. You see before you a wretch, whose life is forfeited. Nay, start not! — the infirmity of my temper has 10 drawn all this misery on me. I left you fretful and passionate — an untoward accident drew me into a quarrel — the event is, that I must fly this kingdom instantly. O Julia, had I been so fortunate as to have called you mine entirely before this mischance had fallen on me, I should not so deeply dread my banishment!

JULIA. My soul is oppressed with sorrow at the nature of your misfortune: had these adverse circumstances arisen from a less fatal cause, I should have felt strong comfort in the thought that I could now chase from your bosom 20 every doubt of the warm sincerity of my love. My heart has long known no other guardian — I now entrust my person to your honour — we will fly together. When safe from pursuit, my father's will may be fulfilled — and I receive a legal claim to be the partner of your sorrows, and tenderest comforter. Then on the bosom of your wedded Julia, you may lull your keen regret to slumbering; while virtuous love, with a cherub's hand, shall smooth the brow of upbraiding thought, and pluck the thorn from compunction. 30

FAULKLAND. O Julia! I am bankrupt in gratitude! but the time is so pressing, it calls on you for so hasty a resolution! — Would you not wish some hours to weigh the advantages you forego, and what little compensation poor Faulkland can make you beside his solitary love?

JULIA. I ask not a moment. No, Faulkland, I have loved you for yourself: and if I now, more than ever, prize the solemn engagement which so long has pledged us to each other, it is because it leaves no room for hard aspersions on my fame, and puts the seal of duty to an act of love. 40 But let us not linger. Perhaps this delay ——

FAULKLAND. 'Twill be better I should not venture out again till dark. Yet am I grieved to think what numberless distresses will press heavy on your gentle disposition!

JULIA. Perhaps your fortune may be forfeited by this unhappy act. I know not whether 'tis so; but sure that alone can never make us unhappy. The little I have will be sufficient to support us; and exile never should be splendid.

50 FAULKLAND. Ay, but in such an abject state of life, my wounded pride perhaps may increase the natural fretfulness of my temper, till I become a rude, morose companion, beyond your patience to endure. Perhaps the recollection of a deed my conscience cannot justify may haunt me in such gloomy and unsocial fits, that I shall hate the tenderness that would relieve me, break from your arms, and quarrel with your fondness!

JULIA. If your thoughts should assume so unhappy a bent, you will the more want some mild and affectionate spirit
60 to watch over and console you: one who, by bearing your infirmities with gentleness and resignation, may teach you so to bear the evils of your fortune.

FAULKLAND. Julia, I have proved you to the quick! and with this useless device I throw away all my doubts. How shall I plead to be forgiven this last unworthy effect of my restless, unsatisfied disposition?

JULIA. Has no such disaster happened as you related?

FAULKLAND. I am ashamed to own that it was pretended; yet in pity, Julia, do not kill me with resenting a fault
70 which never can be repeated: but sealing, this once, my pardon, let me to-morrow, in the face of Heaven, receive my future guide and monitress, and expiate my past folly by years of tender adoration.

JULIA. Hold, Faulkland! — that you are free from a crime, which I before feared to name, Heaven knows how sincerely I rejoice! These are tears of thankfulness for that! But that your cruel doubts should have urged you to an imposition that has wrung my heart, gives me now a pang more keen than I can express!

80 FAULKLAND. By Heavens! Julia ——

JULIA. Yet hear me. — My father loved you, Faulkland!
and you preserved the life that tender parent gave me; in
his presence I pledged my hand — joyfully pledged it —
where before I had given my heart. When, soon after, I
lost that parent, it seemed to me that Providence had, in
Faulkland, shown me whither to transfer, without a
pause, my grateful duty, as well as my affection: hence I
have been content to bear from you what pride and
delicacy would have forbid me from another. I will not
upbraid you, by repeating how you have trifled with my 90
sincerity ——

FAULKLAND. I confess it all! yet hear ——

JULIA. After such a year of trial, I might have flattered
myself that I should not have been insulted with a new
probation of my sincerity, as cruel as unnecessary! I now
see it is not in your nature to be content or confident in
love. With this conviction — I never will be yours. While
I had hopes that my persevering attention, and unre-
proaching kindness, might in time reform your temper,
I should have been happy to have gained a dearer influence 100
over you; but I will not furnish you with a licensed power
to keep alive an incorrigible fault, at the expense of one who
never would contend with you.

FAULKLAND. Nay, but, Julia, by my soul and honour, if
after this ——

JULIA. But one word more. — As my faith has once been
given to you, I never will barter it with another. I shall
pray for your happiness with the truest sincerity; and the
dearest blessing I can ask of Heaven to send you will be to
charm you from that unhappy temper, which alone has 110
prevented the performance of our solemn engagement.
All I request of you is, that you will yourself reflect upon
this infirmity, and when you number up the many true
delights it has deprived you of, let it not be your least

1.95 probation: *trial*.

regret, that it lost you the love of one who would have
followed you in beggary through the world! [*Exit.*

FAULKLAND. She's gone — for ever! — There was an awful
resolution in her manner, that riveted me to my place. —
O fool! — dolt! — barbarian! Cursed as I am, with more
120 imperfections than my fellow-wretches, kind Fortune sent
a heaven-gifted cherub to my aid, and, like a ruffian, I
have driven her from my side! — I must now haste to my
appointment. Well, my mind is tuned for such a scene. I
shall wish only to become a principal in it, and reverse the
tale my cursed folly put me upon forging here. — O love!
— tormentor! — fiend! — whose influence, like the moon's,
acting on men of dull souls, makes idiots of them, but
meeting subtler spirits, betrays their course, and urges
sensibility to madness! [*Exit.*

Enter LYDIA *and* MAID

130 MAID. My mistress, ma'am, I know, was here just now —
perhaps she is only in the next room. [*Exit.*

LYDIA. Heigh-ho! Though he has used me so, this fellow
runs strangely in my head. I believe one lecture from my
grave cousin will make me recall him. [*Re-enter* JULIA.]
O Julia, I am come to you with such an appetite for consolation. — Lud! child, what's the matter with you? You
have been crying! — I'll be hanged if that Faulkland has
not been tormenting you!

JULIA. You mistake the cause of my uneasiness! — Some-
140 thing has flurried me a little. Nothing that you can guess
at. — [*Aside.*] I would not accuse Faulkland to a sister!

LYDIA. Ah! whatever vexations you may have, I can assure
you mine surpass them. You know who Beverley proves
to be?

---

ll.126-7 whose influence, like the moon's, ... makes idiots of them:
lunacy (*Lat.* luna, *the moon*) *was formerly supposed to be greatly
influenced by changes of the moon.*

JULIA. I will now own to you, Lydia, that Mr. Faulkland
had before informed me of the whole affair. Had young
Absolute been the person you took him for, I should not
have accepted your confidence on the subject, without a
serious endeavour to counteract your caprice.

LYDIA. So, then, I see I have been deceived by everyone! 150
But I don't care — I'll never have him.

JULIA. Nay, Lydia ——

LYDIA. Why, is it not provoking? when I thought we were
coming to the prettiest distress imaginable, to find myself
made a mere Smithfield bargain of at last! There had I
projected one of the most sentimental elopements! — so
becoming a disguise! — so amiable a ladder of ropes! —
conscious moon — four horses — Scotch parson — with
such surprise to Mrs. Malaprop — and such paragraphs in
the newspapers! — Oh, I shall die with disappointment! 160

JULIA. I don't wonder at it!

LYDIA. Now — sad reverse! — what have I to expect, but,
after a deal of flimsy preparation with a bishop's licence,
and my aunt's blessing, to go simpering up to the altar; or
perhaps be cried three times in a country church, and have
an unmannerly fat clerk ask the consent of every butcher
in the parish to join John Absolute and Lydia Languish,
spinster! Oh, that I should live to hear myself called
spinster!

JULIA. Melancholy indeed!   170

---

ll.146-9 *i.e. if Captain Absolute had really been Ensign Beverley,
Julia would have considered that she ought to do something to stop
the love affair.*
l.155 Smithfield bargain: *the London meat market; in 1775 also a
cattle market.*
l.158 Scotch parson: *a reference to the famous tendency of runaway
English couples to make for Scotland, where the marriage laws are
different and less exacting.*

LYDIA. How mortifying, to remember the dear delicious shifts I used to be put to, to gain half a minute's conversation with this fellow! How often have I stole forth, in the coldest night in January, and found him in the garden, stuck like a dripping statue! There would he kneel to me in the snow, and sneeze and cough so pathetically! he shivering with cold and I with apprehension! and while the freezing blast numbed our joints, how warmly would he press me to pity his flame, and glow with mutual
180 ardour! — Ah, Julia, that was something like being in love.

JULIA. If I were in spirits, Lydia, I should chide you only by laughing heartily at you; but it suits more the situation of my mind, at present, earnestly to entreat you not to let a man, who loves you with sincerity, suffer that unhappiness from your caprice, which I know too well caprice can inflict.

LYDIA. O Lud! what has brought my aunt here?

Enter MRS. MALAPROP, FAG, *and* DAVID

MRS. MALAPROP. So! so! here's fine work! — here's fine suicide, parricide, and simulation, going on in the fields!
190 and Sir Anthony not to be found to prevent the antistrophe!

JULIA. For Heaven's sake, madam, what's the meaning of this?

MRS. MALAPROP. That gentleman can tell you — 'twas he enveloped the affair to me.

LYDIA. [*To* FAG]. Do, sir, will you, inform us?

FAG. Ma'am, I should hold myself very deficient in every requisite that forms the man of breeding, if I delayed a moment to give all the information in my power to a lady
200 so deeply interested in the affair as you are.

LYDIA. But quick! quick, sir!

FAG. True, ma'am, as you say, one should be quick in divulging matters of this nature; for should we be tedious, perhaps while we are flourishing on the subject, two or three lives may be lost!

LYDIA. O patience! — Do, ma'am, for Heaven's sake! tell us what is the matter?

MRS. MALAPROP. Why, murder's the matter! slaughter's the matter! killing's the matter! — but he can tell you the perpendiculars. 210

LYDIA. Then, prithee, sir, be brief.

FAG. Why then, ma'am, as to murder — I cannot take upon me to say — and as to slaughter, or manslaughter, that will be as the jury finds it.

LYDIA. But who, sir — who are engaged in this?

FAG. Faith, ma'am, one is a young gentleman whom I should be very sorry anything was to happen to — a very pretty behaved gentleman! We have lived much together, and always on terms.

LYDIA. But who is this? who! who! who! 220

FAG. My master, ma'am — my master — I speak of my master.

LYDIA. Heavens! What, Captain Absolute!

MRS. MALAPROP. Oh, to be sure, you are frightened now!

JULIA. But who are with him, sir?

FAG. As to the rest, ma'am, this gentleman can inform you better than I.

JULIA. [To DAVID]. Do speak, friend.

DAVID. Look'ee, my lady — by the mass! there's mischief going on. Folks don't use to meet for amusement with 230 firearms, firelocks, fire-engines, fire-screens, fire-office, and the devil knows what other crackers beside! — This, my lady, I say, has an angry favour.

---

l.231 firelock: *an old type of gun.*
l.233 favour: *appearance.*

JULIA. But who is there beside Captain Absolute, friend?

DAVID. My poor master — under favour for mentioning him first. You know me, my lady — I am David — and my master of course is, or was, Squire Acres. Then comes Squire Faulkland.

JULIA. Do, ma'am, let us instantly endeavour to prevent
240 mischief.

MRS. MALAPROP. O fie! — it would be very inelegant in us: — we should only participate things.

DAVID. Ah! do, Mrs. Aunt, save a few lives — they are desperately given, believe me. — Above all, there is that bloodthirsty Philistine, Sir Lucius O'Trigger.

MRS. MALAPROP. Sir Lucius O'Trigger? O mercy! have they drawn poor little dear Sir Lucius into the scrape? — Why, how you stand, girl! you have no more feeling than one of the Derbyshire petrifactions!

250 LYDIA. What are we to do, madam?

MRS. MALAPROP. Why, fly with the utmost felicity, to be sure, to prevent mischief! — Here, friend, you can show us the place?

FAG. If you please, ma'am, I will conduct you. — David, do you look for Sir Anthony. [*Exit* DAVID.

MRS. MALAPROP. Come, girls! this gentleman will exhort us. — Come, sir, you're our envoy — lead the way, and we'll precede.

FAG. Not a step before the ladies for the world!

260 MRS. MALAPROP. You're sure you know the spot?

---

l.235 under favour for: *excuse me for.*
l.245 bloodthirsty Philistine: *a symbol for ferocity drawn from the Bible. In Sheridan's day the word had not yet acquired the meaning of uncivilized boor.*
l.249 the Derbyshire petrifactions: *in certain places in Derbyshire objects placed under dripping water containing a high proportion of lime become covered with a deposit resembling stone.*

FAG. I think I can find it, ma'am; and one good thing is, we shall hear the report of the pistols as we draw near, so we can't well miss them; — never fear, ma'am, never fear.

> [*Exeunt, he talking.*]

SCENE II. *The South Parade*

Enter CAPTAIN ABSOLUTE, *putting his sword under his great coat*

ABSOLUTE. — A sword seen in the streets of Bath would raise as great an alarm as a mad dog. — How provoking this is in Faulkland! — never punctual! I shall be obliged to go without him at last. — Oh, here's Sir Anthony! how shall I escape him?

> [*Muffles up his face, and takes a circle to go off.*]

Enter SIR ANTHONY ABSOLUTE

SIR ANTHONY. How one may be deceived at a little distance! only that I see he don't know me, I could have sworn that was Jack! — Hey! Gad's life! it is. — Why, Jack, what are you afraid of? hey! — sure I'm right. — Why Jack, Jack Absolute!   [*Goes up to him.* 10

ABSOLUTE. Really, sir, you have the advantage of me: — I don't remember ever to have had the honour — my name is Saunderson, at your service.

SIR ANTHONY. Sir, I beg your pardon — I took you — hey? — why, zounds! it is — Stay — [*Looks up to his face.*] So, so — your humble servant, Mr. Saunderson! Why, you scoundrel, what tricks are you after now?

ABSOLUTE. Oh, a joke, sir, a joke! I came here on purpose to look for you, sir.

SIR ANTHONY. You did! well, I am glad you were so lucky: 20 — but what are you muffled up so for? — what's this for? — hey!

ABSOLUTE. 'Tis cool, sir; isn't? — rather chilly somehow; — but I shall be late — I have a particular engagement.

SIR ANTHONY. Stay! — Why, I thought you were looking
for me? — Pray, Jack, where is't you are going?

ABSOLUTE. Going, sir!

SIR ANTHONY. Ay, where are you going?

ABSOLUTE. Where am I going?

30 SIR ANTHONY. You unmannerly puppy!

ABSOLUTE. I was going, sir, to — to — to — to Lydia — sir,
to Lydia — to make matters up if I could; — and I was
looking for you, sir, to — to —

SIR ANTHONY. To go with you, I suppose. — Well, come
along.

ABSOLUTE. Oh! zounds! no, sir, not for the world! — I
wished to meet with you, sir, — to — to — to — You find it
cool, I'm sure, sir — you'd better not stay out.

SIR ANTHONY. Cool! — not at all. — Well, Jack — and what
40 will you say to Lydia?

ABSOLUTE. Oh, sir, beg her pardon, humour her — promise
and vow: but I detain you, sir — consider the cold air on
your gout.

SIR ANTHONY. Oh, not at all! — not at all! I'm in no hurry.
— Ah! Jack, you youngsters, when once you are wounded
here [*Putting his hand to* CAPTAIN ABSOLUTE'S *breast*].
Hey! what the deuce have you got here?

ABSOLUTE. Nothing, sir — nothing.

SIR ANTHONY. What's this? — here's something hard.

50 ABSOLUTE. Oh, trinkets, sir! trinkets! — a bauble for
Lydia!

SIR ANTHONY. Nay, let me see your taste. — [*Pulls his coat
open, the sword falls.*] Trinkets! — a bauble for Lydia! —
Zounds! sirrah, you are not going to cut her throat, are
you?

ABSOLUTE. Ha! ha! ha! — I thought it would divert you,
sir, though I didn't mean to tell you till afterwards.

SIR ANTHONY. You didn't? — Yes, this is a very diverting trinket, truly!

ABSOLUTE. Sir, I'll explain to you. — You know, sir, Lydia 60 is romantic, devilish romantic, and very absurd of course: now, sir, I intend, if she refuses to forgive me, to unsheath this sword, and swear I'll fall upon its point, and expire at her feet!

SIR ANTHONY. Fall upon a fiddlestick's end! — why, I suppose it is the very thing that would please her. — Get along, you fool!

ABSOLUTE. Well, sir, you shall hear of my success — you shall hear. — *O Lydia!* — *forgive me, or this pointed steel* — says I.   70

SIR ANTHONY. *O booby! stab away and welcome* — says she. — Get along!   [*Exit* CAPTAIN ABSOLUTE.

Enter DAVID, *running*

DAVID. Stop him! stop him! Murder! Thief! Fire! — Stop fire! Stop fire! — O Sir Anthony — call! call! bid'm stop! Murder! Fire!

SIR ANTHONY. Fire! Murder! — Where?

DAVID. Oons! he's out of sight! and I'm out of breath, for my part! O Sir Anthony, why didn't you stop him? why didn't you stop him?

SIR ANTHONY. Zounds! the fellow's mad! — Stop whom? 80 stop Jack?

DAVID. Ay, the captain, sir! — There's murder and slaughter.

SIR ANTHONY. Murder!

DAVID. Ay, please you, Sir Anthony, there's all kinds of murder, all sorts of slaughter to be seen in the fields: there's fighting going on, sir — bloody sword-and-gun fighting!

SIR ANTHONY. Who are going to fight, dunce?

90 DAVID. Everybody that I know of, Sir Anthony — everybody is going to fight, my poor master, Sir Lucius O'Trigger, your son, the captain ——

SIR ANTHONY. Oh, the dog! I see his tricks. — Do you know the place?

DAVID. King's-Mead-Fields.

SIR ANTHONY. You know the way?

DAVID. Not an inch; but I'll call the mayor — aldermen — constables — churchwardens — and beadles — we can't be too many to part them.

100 SIR ANTHONY. Come along — give me your shoulder! we'll get assistance as we go — the lying villain! — Well, I shall be in such a frenzy! — So — this was the history of his trinkets! I'll bauble him! [*Exeunt.*

SCENE III. *King's-Mead-Fields*

Enter SIR LUCIUS O'TRIGGER *and* ACRES, *with pistols*

ACRES. By my valour! then, Sir Lucius, forty yards is a good distance. Odds levels and aims! — I say it is a good distance.

SIR LUCIUS. Is it for muskets or small field-pieces? Upon my conscience, Mr. Acres, you must leave those things to me. — Stay now — I'll show you. — [*Measures paces along the stage.*] There now, that is a very pretty distance — a pretty gentleman's distance.

ACRES. Zounds! we might as well fight in a sentry-box! I
10 tell you, Sir Lucius, the farther he is off, the cooler I shall take my aim.

SIR LUCIUS. Faith! then I suppose you would aim at him best of all if he was out of sight!

ACRES. No, Sir Lucius; but I should think forty or eight-and-thirty yards ——

---

l.98 beadles: *a parish officer whose duty was to preserve order in church, attend on the clergy, and chastise petty offenders.*

SIR LUCIUS. Pho! pho! nonsense! three or four feet between the mouths of your pistols is as good as a mile.

ACRES. Odds bullets, no! — by my valour! there is no merit in killing him so near: do, my dear Sir Lucius, let me bring him down at a long shot: — a long shot, Sir Lucius, 20 if you love me!

SIR LUCIUS. Well, the gentleman's friend and I must settle that. — But tell me now, Mr. Acres, in case of an accident, is there any little will or commission I could execute for you?

ACRES. I am much obliged to you, Sir Lucius — but I don't understand —

SIR LUCIUS. Why, you may think there's no being shot at without a little risk — and if an unlucky bullet should carry a quietus with it — I say it will be no time then to be 30 bothering you about family matters.

ACRES. A quietus!

SIR LUCIUS. For instance, now — if that should be the case — would you choose to be pickled and sent home? — or would it be the same to you to lie here in the Abbey! — I'm told there is very snug lying in the Abbey.

ACRES. Pickled! — Snug lying in the Abbey! — Odds tremors! Sir Lucius, don't talk so!

SIR LUCIUS. I suppose, Mr. Acres, you never were engaged in an affair of this kind before?   40

ACRES. No, Sir Lucius, never before.

SIR LUCIUS. Ah! that's a pity! — there's nothing like being used to a thing. — Pray now, how would you receive the gentleman's shot?

---

l.30 a quietus: *i.e. death. See* Hamlet, *III. i.* 73, 74.
l.35 in the Abbey: *the great Abbey Church at Bath.*

ACRES. Odds files! — I've practised that — there, Sir Lucius — there. [*Puts himself in an attitude.*] A side-front, hey? Odd! I'll make myself small enough: I'll stand edgeways.

SIR LUCIUS. Now — you're quite out — for if you stand so when I take my aim —— [*Levelling at him.*

50 ACRES. Zounds! Sir Lucius — are you sure it is not cocked?

SIR LUCIUS. Never fear.

ACRES. But — but — you don't know — it may go off of its own head!

SIR LUCIUS. Pho! be easy. — Well, now if I hit you in the body, my bullet has a double chance — for if it misses a vital part of your right side — 'twill be very hard if it don't succeed on the left!

ACRES. A vital part?

SIR LUCIUS. But, there — fix yourself so — [*Placing him.*] —
60 let him see the broad-side of your full front — there — now a ball or two may pass clean through your body, and never do any harm at all.

ACRES. Clean through me! — a ball or two clean through me!

SIR LUCIUS. Ay, may they — and it is much the genteelest attitude into the bargain.

ACRES. Look'ee! Sir Lucius — I'd just as lief be shot in an awkward posture as a genteel one; so, by my valour! I will stand edgeways.

SIR LUCIUS. [*Looking at his watch*]. Sure they don't mean to
70 disappoint us — Hah! — no, faith — I think I see them coming.

ACRES. Hey! — what! — coming! ——

SIR LUCIUS. Ay. — Who are those yonder getting over the stile?

ACRES. There are two of them indeed! — well — let them come — hey, Sir Lucius! — we — we — we — we — won't run.

SIR LUCIUS. Run!

ACRES. No — I say — we won't run, by my valour!

SIR LUCIUS. What the devil's the matter with you?   80

ACRES. Nothing — nothing — my dear friend — my dear Sir Lucius — but I — I — I don't feel quite so bold, somehow, as I did.

SIR LUCIUS. O fie! — consider your honour.

ACRES. Ay — true — my honour. Do, Sir Lucius, edge in a word or two every now and then about my honour.

SIR LUCIUS. [*Looking*]. Well, here they're coming.

ACRES. Sir Lucius — if I wa'n't with you, I should almost think I was afraid. — If my valour should leave me! — Valour will come and go.   90

SIR LUCIUS. Then pray keep it fast, while you have it.

ACRES. Sir Lucius — I doubt it is going — yes — my valour is certainly going! — it is sneaking off! — I feel it oozing out as it were at the palms of my hands!

SIR LUCIUS. Your honour — your honour! — Here they are.

ACRES. O mercy! — now — that I was safe at Clod-Hall! or could be shot before I was aware!

Enter FAULKLAND *and* CAPTAIN ABSOLUTE

SIR LUCIUS. Gentlemen, your most obedient. — Hah! — what, Captain Absolute! — So, I suppose, sir, you are come here, just like myself — to do a kind office, first for 100 your friend — then to proceed to business on your own account.

ACRES. What, Jack! — my dear Jack! — my dear friend!

ABSOLUTE. Hark'ee, Bob, Beverley's at hand.

SIR LUCIUS. Well, Mr. Acres — I don't blame your saluting the gentleman civilly. [*To* FAULKLAND.] So, Mr. Beverley, if you'll choose your weapons, the captain and I will measure the ground.

FAULKLAND. My weapons, sir!

110 ACRES. Odds life! Sir Lucius, I'm not going to fight Mr. Faulkland; these are my particular friends.

SIR LUCIUS. What, sir, did you not come here to fight Mr. Acres?

FAULKLAND. Not I, upon my word, sir.

SIR LUCIUS. Well, now, that's mighty provoking! But I hope, Mr. Faulkland, as there are three of us come on purpose for the game, you won't be so cantankerous as to spoil the party by sitting out.

ABSOLUTE. O pray, Faulkland, fight to oblige Sir Lucius.

120 FAULKLAND. Nay, if Mr. Acres is so bent on the matter——

ACRES. No, no, Mr. Faulkland; — I'll bear my disappointment like a Christian. — Look'ee, Sir Lucius, there's no occasion at all for me to fight; and if it is the same to you, I'd as lief let it alone.

SIR LUCIUS. Observe me, Mr. Acres — I must not be trifled with. You have certainly challenged somebody — and you came here to fight him. Now, if that gentleman is willing to represent him, I can't see, for my soul, why it isn't just the same thing.

130 ACRES. Why no — Sir Lucius — I tell you, 'tis one Beverley I've challenged — a fellow, you see, that dare not show his face! — If he were here, I'd make him give up his pretensions directly.

ABSOLUTE. Hold, Bob — let me set you right — there is no such man as Beverley in the case. — The person who assumed that name is before you; and as his pretensions are the same in both characters, he is ready to support them in whatever way you please.

SIR LUCIUS. Well, this is lucky. — Now you have an oppor-
140 tunity——

ACRES. What, quarrel with my dear friend Jack Absolute? — not if he were fifty Beverleys! Zounds! Sir Lucius, you would not have me so unnatural.

SIR LUCIUS. Upon my conscience, Mr. Acres, your valour has oozed away with a vengeance!

ACRES. Not in the least! Odds backs and abettors! I'll be your second with all my heart — and if you should get a quietus, you may command me entirely. I'll get you snug lying in the Abbey here; or pickle you, and send you over to Blunderbuss-hall, or anything of the kind, with the 150 greatest pleasure.

SIR LUCIUS. Pho! pho! you are little better than a coward.

ACRES. Mind, gentlemen, he calls me a coward; coward was the word, by my valour!

SIR LUCIUS. Well, sir?

ACRES. Look'ee, Sir Lucius, 'tisn't that I mind the word coward — coward may be said in joke — but if you had called me a poltroon, odds daggers and balls ——

SIR LUCIUS. Well, sir?

ACRES. I should have thought you a very ill-bred man.   160

SIR LUCIUS. Pho! you are beneath my notice.

ABSOLUTE. Nay, Sir Lucius, you can't have a better second than my friend Acres. — He is a most determined dog — called in the country, Fighting Bob. — He generally kills a man a week — don't you, Bob?

ACRES. Ay — at home!

SIR LUCIUS. Well, then, captain, 'tis we must begin — so come out, my little counsellor — [draws his sword] — and ask the gentleman, whether he will resign the lady, without forcing you to proceed against him?   170

ABSOLUTE. Come on then, sir — [draws]; since you won't let it be an amicable suit, here's my reply.

Enter SIR ANTHONY ABSOLUTE, DAVID, MRS. MALAPROP, LYDIA, *and* JULIA

1.146 backs and abettors: *those who back or second one in an enterprise.*

DAVID. Knock 'em all down, sweet Sir Anthony; knock down my master in particular; and bind his hands over to their good behaviour!

SIR ANTHONY. Put up, Jack, put up, or I shall be in a frenzy — how came you in a duel, sir?

ABSOLUTE. Faith, sir, that gentleman can tell you better than I; 'twas he called on me, and you know, sir, I serve
180 his majesty.

SIR ANTHONY. Here's a pretty fellow; I catch him going to cut a man's throat, and he tells me, he serves his majesty! — Zounds! sirrah, then how durst you draw the king's sword against one of his subjects?

ABSOLUTE. Sir, I tell you! that gentleman called me out, without explaining his reasons.

SIR ANTHONY. Gad! sir, how came you to call my son out, without explaining your reasons?

SIR LUCIUS. Your son, sir, insulted me in a manner which
190 my honour would not brook.

SIR ANTHONY. Zounds! Jack, how durst you insult the gentleman in a manner which his honour could not brook?

MRS. MALAPROP. Come, come, let's have no honour before ladies. — Captain Absolute, come here — How could you intimidate us so? — Here's Lydia has been terrified to death for you.

ABSOLUTE. For fear I should be killed, or escape, ma'am?

MRS. MALAPROP. Nay, no delusions to the past — Lydia is convinced; speak, child.

200 SIR LUCIUS. With your leave, ma'am, I must put in a word here: I believe I could interpret the young lady's silence. Now mark ——

LYDIA. What is it you mean, sir?

SIR LUCIUS. Come, come, Delia, we must be serious now — this is no time for trifling.

LYDIA. 'Tis true, sir; and your reproof bids me offer this gentleman my hand, and solicit the return of his affections.

ABSOLUTE. O! my little angel, say you so! — Sir Lucius — I perceive there must be some mistake here, with regard to the affront which you affirm I have given you. I can only 210 say, that it could not have been intentional. And as you must be convinced, that I should not fear to support a real injury, you shall now see that I am not ashamed to atone for an inadvertency — I ask your pardon. — But for this lady, while honoured with her approbation, I will support my claim against any man whatever.

SIR ANTHONY. Well said, Jack, and I'll stand by you, my boy.

ACRES. Mind, I give up all my claim — I make no pretensions to anything in the world; and if I can't get a wife 220 without fighting for her, by my valour! I'll live a bachelor.

SIR LUCIUS. Captain, give me your hand: an affront handsomely acknowledged becomes an obligation; and as for the lady, if she chooses to deny her own hand-writing, here —   [*Takes out letters.*

MRS. MALAPROP. O, he will dissolve my mystery! — Sir Lucius, perhaps there's some mistake — perhaps I can illuminate —

SIR LUCIUS. Pray, old gentlewoman, don't interfere where you have no business. — Miss Languish, are you my Delia, 230 or not?

LYDIA. Indeed, Sir Lucius, I am not.
                    [*Walks aside with* CAPTAIN ABSOLUTE.

MRS. MALAPROP. Sir Lucius O'Trigger — ungrateful as you are — I own the soft impeachment — pardon my blushes, I am Delia.

SIR LUCIUS. You Delia — pho! pho! be easy.

---

l.214 inadvertency: *mistake.*

MRS. MALAPROP. Why, thou barbarous Vandyke — those
letters are mine — When you are more sensible of my
benignity — perhaps I may be brought to encourage your
240   addresses.

SIR LUCIUS. Mrs. Malaprop, I am extremely sensible of your
condescension; and whether you or Lucy have put this
trick on me, I am equally beholden to you. — And, to
show you I am not ungrateful, Captain Absolute, since
you have taken that lady from me, I'll give you my Delia
into the bargain.

ABSOLUTE. I am much obliged to you, Sir Lucius; but here's
my friend, Fighting Bob, unprovided for.

SIR LUCIUS. Hah! little Valour — here, will you make your
250   fortune?

ACRES. Odds wrinkles! No. — But give me your hand, Sir
Lucius, forget and forgive; but if ever I give you a chance
of pickling me again, say Bob Acres is a dunce, that's all.

SIR ANTHONY. Come, Mrs. Malaprop, don't be cast down
— you are in your bloom yet.

MRS. MALAPROP. O Sir Anthony — men are all barbarians.
[*All retire but* JULIA *and* FAULKLAND.

JULIA. [*Aside*]. He seems dejected and unhappy — not
sullen; there was some foundation, however, for the tale
he told me — O woman! how true should be your judg-
260   ment, when your resolution is so weak!

FAULKLAND. Julia! — how can I sue for what I so little
deserve? I dare not presume — yet Hope is the child of
Penitence.

JULIA. O! Faulkland, you have not been more faulty in
your unkind treatment of me, than I am now in wanting
inclination to resent it. As my heart honestly bids me
place my weakness to the account of love, I should be ungenerous not to admit the same plea for yours.

---

l.237 Vandyke: *for Vandal.*

FAULKLAND. Now I shall be blest indeed!

SIR ANTHONY. [*Coming forward*]. What's going on here? — 270
So you have been quarrelling too, I warrant! Come, Julia,
I never interfered before; but let me have a hand in the
matter at last. — All the faults I have ever seen in my
friend Faulkland seemed to proceed from what he calls
the delicacy and warmth of his affection for you — There,
marry him directly, Julia; you'll find he'll mend surprisingly!   [*The rest come forward.*

SIR LUCIUS. Come, now, I hope there is no dissatisfied person, but what is content; for as I have been disappointed
myself, it will be very hard if I have not the satisfaction of 280
seeing other people succeed better.

ACRES. You are right, Sir Lucius. — So, Jack, I wish you joy
— Mr. Faulkland the same. — Ladies, — come now, to
show you I'm neither vexed nor angry, odds tabors and
pipes! I'll order the fiddles in half an hour to the New
Rooms — and I insist on your all meeting me there.

SIR ANTHONY. 'Gad! sir, I like your spirit; and at night we
single lads will drink a health to the young couples, and a
husband to Mrs. Malaprop.

FAULKLAND. Our partners are stolen from us, Jack — I hope 290
to be congratulated by each other — yours for having
checked in time the errors of an ill-directed imagination,
which might have betrayed an innocent heart; and mine,
for having, by her gentleness and candour, reformed the
unhappy temper of one, who by it made wretched whom he
loved most, and tortured the heart he ought to have
adored.

ABSOLUTE. Well, Jack, we have both tasted the bitters, as
well as the sweets of love; with this difference only, that
you always prepared the bitter cup for yourself, while I —— 300

ll.284-5 tabors and pipes: *see note on p.57.*
ll.285-6 the New Rooms: *an exclusive assembly room in Bath.*

LYDIA. Was always obliged to me for it, hey! Mr. Modesty? — But, come, no more of that — our happiness is now as unalloyed as general.

JULIA. Then let us study to preserve it so: and while Hope pictures to us a flattering scene of future bliss, let us deny its pencil those colours which are too bright to be lasting. — When hearts deserving happiness would unite their fortunes, Virtue would crown them with an unfading garland of modest hurtless flowers; but ill-judging Passion will 310 force the gaudier rose into the wreath, whose thorn offends them when its leaves are dropped! [*Exeunt All.*

The School for Scandal

INTRODUCTION

The School for Scandal, produced in the spring of 1777, was enthusiastically received. Even when its first run was over it continued to be by far the most popular of revivals. In 1779 the Treasurer to Drury Lane noted on his official receipts '*School for Scandal* damped the new pieces'.

The play is not profound, nor is it strikingly original, but it is perhaps the most brilliant and most theatrically effective of all English comedies. Sheridan liked the legend to be circulated that he dashed off the manuscript with reckless haste and consummate ease. In point of fact, when he was actually at work, he toiled as assiduously as Horace at an Ode. The concise felicity of expression and the neatness of repartee, which make the dialogue of *The School for Scandal* sparkle like diamonds, can no more be achieved spontaneously than a jig-saw puzzle can be assembled without labour.

'*Sir Peter:* Ah, Madam, true wit is more nearly allied to good nature than your ladyship is aware of.
'*Lady Teazle:* True, Sir Peter; I believe they are so near akin that they can never be united.
'*Sir Benjamin Backbite:* Or rather suppose them man and wife, because one seldom sees them together.'

Was the author of *The School for Scandal* a genius, or merely a brilliant workman? The play certainly throws no new and startling light on human nature or philosophy. So far from rubbing our eyes and saying, 'I never thought of that before', we are more apt to recognize 'That is how I have always known things to be'. It is common knowledge that an extravagant sportsman like Charles Surface is more likely to be warm-hearted than a man as seemingly correct and sententious as his brother. When an old bachelor marries a young wife, the world has long ago learned to look for trouble. A Semitic money-lender like Moses is a by-word for rapacity, and the character of Trip is proverbial — 'like master like man'.

Sheridan has made the play from the very commonest of ingredients. Who could not do the same? To be Shakespeare one must have intuition and inspiration; but why cannot any perceptive man with literary ability (and there have been many such since 1777) repeat the triumph of *The School for Scandal*? The explanation is that the commonness of the ingredients of *The School for Scandal* is the very source of its strength. When all is abnormally said and done, the world always comes back to take interest in the normal actions of human nature, which, as human nature does not change, make their appeal as effectively to one generation as to another.

The Restoration Comedy is neglected because it is really unkind. *The School for Scandal* still flourishes because the unkindness is only pretence, and the audience is intended to disperse with the resolution of Sir Peter 'to live as happily together as Lady Teazle and I intend to do'.

In 1789 the storm of the French Revolution burst. The exquisite, indolent persons of Sheridan's comedy, with all the day before them in which to sip chocolate and exchange raillery amid dazzling surroundings, seem almost like fools enjoying the last hours of their paradise. The storm broke, tried their nerves, sobered their finery, but passed them by. Had they still been reflections of a society as really inhuman as that of the Restoration, it is probable that Madame Guillotine, a lady with an even sharper tongue than Lady Sneerwell's, would have silenced the company.

THE CAST

SIR PETER TEAZLE

SIR OLIVER SURFACE, *a rich East India merchant*

SIR HARRY BUMPER, *roystering friend of Charles Surface*

SIR BENJAMIN BACKBITE, *a man of fashion*

JOSEPH SURFACE
CHARLES SURFACE } *Sir Oliver's nephews*

CARELESS, *friend of Charles Surface*

SNAKE, *friend and confidant to Lady Sneerwell*

CRABTREE, *uncle to Sir Benjamin*

ROWLEY, *Sir Peter's friend*

MOSES, *a Jewish financier*

TRIP, *servant to Charles Surface*

LADY TEAZLE, *wife to Sir Peter*

LADY SNEERWELL
MRS. CANDOUR } *Ladies of fashion*

MARIA, *Sir Peter's ward*

GENTLEMEN, MAID AND SERVANTS

Scene: Fashionable London in 1777

ACT I

Scene I. *Lady Sneerwell's Dressing-room*

LADY SNEERWELL *discovered at her toilet*; SNAKE *drinking chocolate*

LADY SNEERWELL. The paragraphs, you say, Mr. Snake, were all inserted?

SNAKE. They were, madam; and, as I copied them myself in a feigned hand, there can be no suspicion whence they came.

LADY SNEERWELL. Did you circulate the report of Lady Brittle's intrigue with Captain Boastall?

SNAKE. That's in as fine a train as your ladyship could wish. In the common course of things, I think it must reach Mrs. Clackitt's ears within four-and-twenty hours; and 10 then, you know, the business is as good as done.

LADY SNEERWELL. Why, truly, Mrs. Clackitt has a very pretty talent, and a great deal of industry.

SNAKE. True, madam, and has been tolerably successful in her day. To my knowledge, she has been the cause of six matches being broken off, and three sons being disinherited; of four forced elopements, nine separate maintenances, and two divorces. Nay, I have more than once traced her causing a *tête-à-tête* in the 'Town and Country Magazine', when the parties, perhaps, had never seen each 20 other's face before in the course of their lives.

LADY SNEERWELL. She certainly has talents, but her manner is gross.

SNAKE. 'Tis very true. She generally designs well, has a free tongue and a bold invention; but her colouring is too dark, and her outlines often extravagant. She wants that

---

It was common in the eighteenth century for male friends and admirers to attend ladies of fashion while they dressed, an operation which took a long time.

delicacy of tint, and mellowness of sneer, which distinguish your ladyship's scandal.

LADY SNEERWELL. You are partial, Snake.

30 SNAKE. Not in the least; everybody allows that Lady Sneerwell can do more with a word or look than many can with the most laboured detail, even when they happen to have a little truth on their side to support it.

LADY SNEERWELL. Yes, my dear Snake; and I am no hypocrite to deny the satisfaction I reap from the success of my efforts. Wounded myself, in the early part of my life, by the envenomed tongue of slander, I confess I have since known no pleasure equal to the reducing others to the level of my own reputation.

40 SNAKE. Nothing can be more natural. But, Lady Sneerwell, there is one affair in which you have lately employed me, wherein, I confess, I am at a loss to guess your motives.

LADY SNEERWELL. I conceive you mean with respect to my neighbour, Sir Peter Teazle, and his family?

SNAKE. I do. Here are two young men, to whom Sir Peter has acted as a kind of guardian since their father's death; the eldest possessing the most amiable character, and universally well spoken of — the youngest, the most dissipated and extravagant young fellow in the kingdom, with-
50 out friends or character: the former an avowed admirer of your ladyship, and apparently your favourite; the latter attached to Maria, Sir Peter's ward, and confessedly beloved by her. Now, on the face of these circumstances, it is utterly unaccountable to me, why you, the widow of a city knight, with a good jointure, should not close with the passion of a man of such character and expectations as Mr. Surface; and more so why you should be so uncommonly earnest to destroy the mutual attachment subsisting between his brother Charles and Maria.

60 LADY SNEERWELL. Then, at once to unravel this mystery, I must inform you that love has no share whatever in the intercourse between Mr. Surface and me.

SNAKE. No!

LADY SNEERWELL. His real attachment is to Maria, or her fortune; but, finding in his brother a favoured rival, he has been obliged to mask his pretensions, and profit by my assistance.

SNAKE. Yet still I am more puzzled why you should interest yourself in his success.

LADY SNEERWELL. Heavens! how dull you are! Cannot you 70 surmise the weakness which I hitherto, through shame, have concealed even from you? Must I confess that Charles — that extravagant, that bankrupt in fortune and reputation — that he it is for whom I am thus anxious and malicious, and to gain whom I would sacrifice everything?

SNAKE. Now, indeed, your conduct appears consistent: but how came you and Mr. Surface so confidential?

LADY SNEERWELL. For our mutual interest. I have found him out a long time since. I know him to be artful, selfish, and malicious — in short, a sentimental knave; while with 80 Sir Peter, and indeed with all his acquaintance, he passes for a youthful miracle of prudence, good sense, and benevolence.

SNAKE. Yes; yet Sir Peter vows he has not his equal in England; and, above all, he praises him as a man of sentiment.

LADY SNEERWELL. True; and with the assistance of his sentiment and hypocrisy he has brought Sir Peter entirely into his interest with regard to Maria; while poor Charles has no friend in the house — though, I fear, he has a 90 powerful one in Maria's heart, against whom we must direct our schemes.

Enter SERVANT

SERVANT. Mr. Surface.

1.85 sentiment: *of sensitive and civilized feelings.*

LADY SNEERWELL. Show him up. [*Exit* SERVANT.] He generally calls about this time. I don't wonder at people giving him to me for a lover.

Enter JOSEPH SURFACE

JOSEPH SURFACE. My dear Lady Sneerwell, how do you do to-day? Mr. Snake, your most obedient.

LADY SNEERWELL. Snake has just been rallying me on our mutual attachment, but I have informed him of our real views. You know how useful he has been to us; and, believe me, the confidence is not ill-placed.

JOSEPH SURFACE. Madam, it is impossible for me to suspect a man of Mr. Snake's sensibility and discernment.

LADY SNEERWELL. Well, well, no compliments now; but tell me when you saw your mistress, Maria — or, what is more material to me, your brother.

JOSEPH SURFACE. I have not seen either since I left you, but I can inform you that they never meet. Some of your stories have taken a good effect on Maria.

LADY SNEERWELL. Ah, my dear Snake! the merit of this belongs to you. But do your brother's distresses increase?

JOSEPH SURFACE. Every hour. I am told he has had another execution in the house yesterday. In short, his dissipation and extravagance exceed anything I have ever heard of.

LADY SNEERWELL. Poor Charles!

JOSEPH SURFACE. True, madam; notwithstanding his vices, one can't help feeling for him. Poor Charles! I'm sure I wish it were in my power to be of any essential service to him; for the man who does not share in the distresses of a brother, even though merited by his own misconduct, deserves ——

---

l.104 sensibility: *knowledge of the world.*
l.114 execution in the house: *the modern equivalent would be 'the bailiffs in again'.*

LADY SNEERWELL. O Lud! you are going to be moral, and forget that you are among friends.

JOSEPH SURFACE. Egad, that's true! I'll keep that sentiment till I see Sir Peter. However, it is certainly a charity to rescue Maria from such a man, who if he is to be reclaimed, can be so only by a person of your ladyship's superior accomplishments and understanding.   130

SNAKE. I believe, Lady Sneerwell, here's company coming: I'll go and copy the letter I mentioned to you. Mr. Surface, your most obedient.

JOSEPH SURFACE. Sir, your very devoted. — [*Exit* SNAKE.] Lady Sneerwell, I am very sorry you have put any farther confidence in that fellow.

LADY SNEERWELL. Why so?

JOSEPH SURFACE. I have lately detected him in frequent conference with old Rowley, who was formerly my father's steward, and has never, you know, been a friend of mine.   140

LADY SNEERWELL. And do you think he would betray us?

JOSEPH SURFACE. Nothing more likely: take my word for't, Lady Sneerwell, that fellow hasn't virtue enough to be faithful even to his own villany. Ah, Maria!

Enter MARIA

LADY SNEERWELL. Maria, my dear, how do you do? What's the matter?

MARIA. Oh! there's that disagreeable lover of mine, Sir Benjamin Backbite, has just called at my guardian's, with his odious uncle, Crabtree; so I slipped out, and ran hither to avoid them.   150

LADY SNEERWELL. Is that all?

JOSEPH SURFACE. If my brother Charles has been of the party, madam, perhaps you would not have been so much alarmed.

LADY SNEERWELL. Nay, now you are severe; for I dare swear the truth of the matter is, Maria heard you were here. But, my dear, what has Sir Benjamin done, that you should avoid him so?

MARIA. Oh, he has done nothing — but 'tis for what he has
160 said: his conversation is a perpetual libel on all his acquaintance.

JOSEPH SURFACE. Ay, and the worst of it is, there is no advantage in not knowing him; for he'll abuse a stranger just as soon as his best friend: and his uncle's as bad.

LADY SNEERWELL. Nay, but we should make allowance; Sir Benjamin is a wit and a poet.

MARIA. For my part, I own, madam, wit loses its respect with me, when I see it in company with malice. What do you think, Mr. Surface?

170 JOSEPH SURFACE. Certainly, madam; to smile at the jest which plants a thorn in another's breast is to become a principal in the mischief.

LADY SNEERWELL. Pshaw! there's no possibility of being witty without a little ill nature: the malice of a good thing is the barb that makes it stick. What's your opinion, Mr. Surface?

JOSEPH SURFACE. To be sure, madam; that conversation, where the spirit of raillery is suppressed, will ever appear tedious and insipid.

180 MARIA. Well, I'll not debate how far scandal may be allowable; but in a man, I am sure, it is always contemptible. We have pride, envy, rivalship, and a thousand motives to depreciate each other; but the male slanderer must have the cowardice of a woman before he can traduce one.

Re-enter SERVANT

SERVANT. Madam, Mrs. Candour is below, and, if your ladyship's at leisure, will leave her carriage.

LADY SNEERWELL. Beg her to walk in. — [*Exit* SERVANT.] Now, Maria, here is a character to your taste; for, though Mrs. Candour is a little talkative, everybody allows her to
190 be the best natured and best sort of woman.

MARIA. Yes, with a very gross affectation of good nature and benevolence, she does more mischief than the direct malice of old Crabtree.

JOSEPH SURFACE. I' faith that's true, Lady Sneerwell: whenever I hear the current running against the characters of my friends, I never think them in such danger as when Candour undertakes their defence.

LADY SNEERWELL. Hush! — here she is!

Enter MRS. CANDOUR

MRS. CANDOUR. My dear Lady Sneerwell, how have you been this century? — Mr. Surface, what news do you hear? 200 — though indeed it is no matter, for I think one hears nothing else but scandal.

JOSEPH SURFACE. Just so, indeed, ma'am.

MRS. CANDOUR. Oh, Maria! child, — what, is the whole affair off between you and Charles? His extravagance, I presume — the town talks of nothing else.

MARIA. I am very sorry, ma'am, the town has so little to do.

MRS. CANDOUR. True, true, child: but there's no stopping people's tongues. I own I was hurt to hear it, as I indeed was to learn, from the same quarter, that your guardian, Sir 210 Peter, and Lady Teazle have not agreed lately as well as could be wished.

MARIA. 'Tis strangely impertinent for people to busy themselves so.

MRS. CANDOUR. Very true, child: but what's to be done? People will talk — there's no preventing it. Why, it was but yesterday I was told that Miss Gadabout had eloped with Sir Filigree Flirt. But, Lord! there's no minding what one hears; though, to be sure, I had this from very good authority. 220

MARIA. Such reports are highly scandalous.

MRS. CANDOUR. So they are, child — shameful, shameful! But the world is so censorious, no character escapes. Lord, now who would have suspected your friend, Miss Prim, of an indiscretion? Yet such is the ill nature of people, that they say her uncle stopped her last week, just as she was stepping into the York Mail with her dancing-master.

MARIA. I'll answer for't there are no grounds for that report.

MRS. CANDOUR. Ah, no foundation in the world, I dare swear; no more, probably, than for the story circulated last month, of Mrs. Festino's affair with Colonel Cassino — though, to be sure, that matter was never rightly cleared up.

JOSEPH SURFACE. The licence of invention some people take is monstrous indeed.

MARIA. 'Tis so; but, in my opinion, those who report such things are equally culpable.

MRS. CANDOUR. To be sure they are; tale-bearers are as bad as the tale-makers — 'tis an old observation, and a very true one: but what's to be done, as I said before? how will you prevent people from talking? To-day, Mrs. Clackitt assured me, Mr. and Mrs. Honeymoor were at last become mere man and wife, like the rest of their acquaintance. But, Lord, do you think I would report these things! No, no! tale-bearers, as I said before, are just as bad as the tale-makers.

JOSEPH SURFACE. Ah! Mrs. Candour, if everybody had your forbearance and good nature!

MRS. CANDOUR. I confess, Mr. Surface, I cannot bear to hear people attacked behind their backs; and when ugly circumstances come out against our acquaintance, I own I always love to think the best. By the by, I hope 'tis not true that your brother is absolutely ruined?

JOSEPH SURFACE. I am afraid his circumstances are very bad indeed, ma'am.

1.227 York Mail: *the coach service of that name.*

MRS. CANDOUR. Ah! I heard so — but you must tell him to keep up his spirits; everybody almost is in the same way; Lord Spindle, Sir Thomas Splint, Captain Quinze, and Mr. Nickit — all up, I hear, within this week; so, if Charles is undone, he'll find half his acquaintance ruined too, and 260 that, you know, is a consolation.

JOSEPH SURFACE. Doubtless, ma'am — a very great one.

Re-enter SERVANT

SERVANT. Mr. Crabtree and Sir Benjamin Backbite. [*Exit.*

LADY SNEERWELL. So, Maria, you see your lover pursues you; positively you sha'n't escape.

Enter CRABTREE *and* SIR BENJAMIN BACKBITE

CRABTREE. Lady Sneerwell, I kiss your hand. Mrs. Candour, I don't believe you are acquainted with my nephew, Sir Benjamin Backbite? Egad, ma'am, he has a pretty wit, and is a pretty poet too. Isn't he, Lady Sneerwell?

SIR BENJAMIN. Oh, fie, uncle!   270

CRABTREE. Nay, egad it's true; I back him at a rebus or a charade against the best rhymer in the kingdom. Has your ladyship heard the epigram he wrote last week on Lady Frizzle's feather catching fire? — Do, Benjamin, repeat it, or the charade you made last night extempore at Mrs. Drowzie's conversazione. Come now; your first is the name of a fish, your second a great naval commander, and ——

SIR BENJAMIN. Uncle, now — pr'ythee ——

CRABTREE. I' faith, ma'am, 'twould surprise you to hear how 280 ready he is at all these sort of things.

---

l.268 pretty: *excellent.*
l.271 rebus: *a popular form of puzzle, as it might be 'crossword'.*
l.272 charade: *a form of word riddle.*
l.276 conversazione: *a party at which clever conversation was expected of the guests.*

LADY SNEERWELL. I wonder, Sir Benjamin, you never publish anything.

SIR BENJAMIN. To say truth, ma'am, 'tis very vulgar to print; and as my little productions are mostly satires and lampoons on particular people, I find they circulate more by giving copies in confidence to the friends of the parties. However, I have some love elegies, which, when favoured with this lady's smiles, I mean to give the public.

[*Pointing to* MARIA.

290 CRABTREE [*to* MARIA]. 'Fore heaven, ma'am, they'll immortalize you! — you will be handed down to posterity, like Petrarch's Laura, or Waller's Sacharissa.

SIR BENJAMIN [*to* MARIA]. Yes, madam, I think you will like them, when you shall see them on a beautiful quarto page, where a neat rivulet of text shall meander through a meadow of margin. 'Fore Gad they will be the most elegant things of their kind!

CRABTREE. But, ladies, that's true — have you heard the news?

300 MRS. CANDOUR. What, sir, do you mean the report of ——

CRABTREE. No, ma'am, that's not it. — Miss Nicely is going to be married to her own footman.

MRS. CANDOUR. Impossible!

CRABTREE. Ask Sir Benjamin.

SIR BENJAMIN. 'Tis very true, ma'am: everything is fixed, and the wedding liveries bespoke.

---

l.285 satires: *literary pieces, generally in verse, with a sarcastic slant.*
l.286 lampoons: *highly malicious compositions, often in song form.*
l.292 Laura *and* Sacharissa: *two famous poetical heroines. The Italian poet Petrarch addressed many sonnets to Laura who may or may not have been a real person. Sacharissa is the name given to the daughter of the Earl of Leicester with whom the poet Edmund Waller was much in love.*
l.294 quarto: *a large, elegant size for a book.*

LADY SNEERWELL. Why, I have heard something of this before.

MRS. CANDOUR. It can't be — and I wonder any one should believe such a story of so prudent a lady as Miss Nicely. 310

SIR BENJAMIN. O Lud! ma'am, that's the very reason 'twas believed at once. She has always been so cautious and so reserved, that everybody was sure there was some reason for it at bottom.

MRS. CANDOUR. Why, to be sure, a tale of scandal is as fatal to the credit of a prudent lady of her stamp as a fever is generally to those of the strongest constitutions. But there is a sort of puny sickly reputation, that is always ailing, yet will outlive the robuster characters of a hundred prudes.

SIR BENJAMIN. True, madam, there are valetudinarians in 320 reputation as well as constitution, who, being conscious of their weak part, avoid the least breath of air, and supply their want of stamina by care and circumspection.

MRS. CANDOUR. Well, but this may be all a mistake. You know, Sir Benjamin, very trifling circumstances often give rise to the most injurious tales.

CRABTREE. That they do, I'll be sworn, ma'am. O Lud! Mr. Surface, pray is it true that your uncle, Sir Oliver, is coming home?

JOSEPH SURFACE. Not that I know of, indeed, sir.   330

CRABTREE. He has been in the East Indies a long time. You can scarcely remember him, I believe? Sad comfort, whenever he returns, to hear how your brother has gone on!

JOSEPH SURFACE. Charles has been imprudent, sir, to be sure; but I hope no busy people have already prejudiced Sir Oliver against him. He may reform.

SIR BENJAMIN. To be sure he may: for my part, I never believed him to be so utterly void of principle as people

---

l.320 valetudinarians: *people who are always thinking they are ill.*

say; and, though he has lost all his friends, I am told no-
340 body is better spoken of by the Jews.

CRABTREE. That's true, egad, nephew. If the Old Jewry was
a ward, I believe Charles would be an alderman: no man
more popular there, 'fore Gad! I hear he pays as many
annuities as the Irish tontine; and that, whenever he is
sick, they have prayers for the recovery of his health in all
the synagogues.

SIR BENJAMIN. Yet no man lives in greater splendour. They
tell me, when he entertains his friends he will sit down to
dinner with a dozen of his own securities; have a score of
350 tradesmen waiting in the antechamber, and an officer
behind every guest's chair.

JOSEPH SURFACE. This may be entertainment to you, gentlemen, but you pay very little regard to the feelings of a
brother.

MARIA. [*Aside*]. Their malice is intolerable! — [*Aloud.*] Lady
Sneerwell, I must wish you a good morning: I'm not very
well.   [*Exit.*

MRS. CANDOUR. O dear! she changes colour very much.

LADY SNEERWELL. Do, Mrs. Candour, follow her: she may
360 want your assistance.

MRS. CANDOUR. That I will, with all my soul, ma'am. —
Poor dear girl, who knows what her situation may be!
                                                        [*Exit.*

---

l.341 Old Jewry: *a part of the City of London originally inhabited
largely by Jews.*
l.342 ward ... alderman: *in the local government of the City of
London the 'aldermen' represent 'wards'.*
l.344 tontine: *a peculiar form of insurance. An annuity is a sum
paid each year under an insurance scheme. Crabtree's point is that
Charles has so many debts to pay off that he is as useful to his debtors
as an annuity scheme.*
l.349 securities: *people who have guaranteed his debts.*
l.350 officer: *a debt-collecting official.*

LADY SNEERWELL. 'Twas nothing but that she could not bear to hear Charles reflected on, notwithstanding their difference.

SIR BENJAMIN. The young lady's *penchant* is obvious.

CRABTREE. But, Benjamin, you must not give up the pursuit for that: follow her, and put her into good humour. Repeat her some of your own verses. Come, I'll assist you.

SIR BENJAMIN. Mr. Surface, I did not mean to hurt you; 370 but depend on't your brother is utterly undone!

CRABTREE. O Lud, ay! undone as ever man was — can't raise a guinea!

SIR BENJAMIN. And everything sold, I'm told, that was movable.

CRABTREE. I have seen one that was at his house. Not a thing left but some empty bottles that were overlooked, and the family pictures, which I believe are framed in the wainscots.

SIR BENJAMIN. [*Going*]. And I'm very sorry also to hear some 380 bad stories against him.

CRABTREE. Oh, he has done many mean things, that's certain.

SIR BENJAMIN. [*Going*]. But, however, as he's your brother —

CRABTREE. We'll tell you all another opportunity.

Exeunt CRABTREE *and* SIR BENJAMIN

LADY SNEERWELL. Ha! ha! 'tis very hard for them to leave a subject they have not quite run down.

JOSEPH SURFACE. And I believe the abuse was no more acceptable to your ladyship than to Maria.

LADY SNEERWELL. I doubt her affections are farther en- 390 gaged than we imagine. But the family are to be here this evening, so you may as well dine where you are, and we

---

1.366 penchant: *inclination*.

shall have an opportunity of observing farther; in the meantime, I'll go and plot mischief, and you shall study sentiment.

[*Exeunt.*

Scene II. *A Room in Sir Peter Teazle's House*

Enter SIR PETER TEAZLE

SIR PETER. When an old bachelor marries a young wife, what is he to expect? 'Tis now six months since Lady Teazle made me the happiest of men — and I have been the most miserable dog ever since! We tiffed a little going to church, and fairly quarrelled before the bells had done ringing. I was more than once nearly choked with gall during the honeymoon, and had lost all comfort in life before my friends had done wishing me joy. Yet I chose with caution — a girl bred wholly in the country, who never knew 10 luxury beyond one silk gown, nor dissipation above the annual gala of a race ball. Yet she now plays her part in all the extravagant fopperies of fashion and the town, with as ready a grace as if she never had seen a bush or a grass-plot out of Grosvenor Square! I am sneered at by all my acquaintance, and paragraphed in the newspapers. She dissipates my fortune, and contradicts all my humours; yet the worst of it is, I doubt I love her, or I should never bear all this. However, I'll never be weak enough to own it.

Enter ROWLEY

ROWLEY. Oh! Sir Peter, your servant: how is it with you, 20 sir?

SIR PETER. Very bad, Master Rowley, very bad. I meet with nothing but crosses and vexations.

ROWLEY. What can have happened since yesterday?

SIR PETER. A good question to a married man!

1.17 I doubt: *I must.*

ROWLEY. Nay, I'm sure, Sir Peter, your lady can't be the cause of your uneasiness.

SIR PETER. Why, has anybody told you she was dead?

ROWLEY. Come, come, Sir Peter, you love her, notwithstanding your tempers don't exactly agree.

SIR PETER. But the fault is entirely hers, Master Rowley. I 30 am, myself, the sweetest-tempered man alive, and hate a teasing temper; and so I tell her a hundred times a day.

ROWLEY. Indeed!

SIR PETER. Ay; and what is very extraordinary, in all our disputes she is always in the wrong! But Lady Sneerwell, and the set she meets at her house, encourage the perverseness of her disposition. Then, to complete my vexation, Maria, my ward, whom I ought to have the power of a father over, is determined to turn rebel too, and absolutely refuses the man whom I have long resolved on for her 40 husband; meaning, I suppose, to bestow herself on his profligate brother.

ROWLEY. You know, Sir Peter, I have always taken the liberty to differ with you on the subject of these two young gentlemen. I only wish you may not be deceived in your opinion of the elder. For Charles, my life on't! he will retrieve his errors yet. Their worthy father, once my honoured master, was, at his years, nearly as wild a spark; yet, when he died, he did not leave a more benevolent heart to lament his loss.   50

SIR PETER. You are wrong, Master Rowley. On their father's death, you know, I acted as a kind of guardian to them both, till their uncle Sir Oliver's liberality gave them an early independence: of course, no person could have more opportunities of judging of their hearts, and I was never mistaken in my life. Joseph is indeed a model for the young men of the age. He is a man of sentiment, and acts

---

1.57 of sentiment: *of kindly feeling for his fellow men.*

up to the sentiments he professes; but, for the other, take my word for't, if he had any grain of virtue by descent, he
60 has dissipated it with the rest of his inheritance. Ah! my old friend, Sir Oliver, will be deeply mortified when he finds how part of his bounty has been misapplied.

ROWLEY. I am sorry to find you so violent against the young man, because this may be the most critical period of his fortune. I came hither with news that will surprise you.

SIR PETER. What! let me hear.

ROWLEY. Sir Oliver is arrived, and at this moment in town.

SIR PETER. How! you astonish me! I thought you did not expect him this month.

70 ROWLEY. I did not: but his passage has been remarkably quick.

SIR PETER. Egad, I shall rejoice to see my old friend. 'Tis sixteen years since we met. We have had many a day together: — but does he still enjoin us not to inform his nephews of his arrival?

ROWLEY. Most strictly. He means, before it is known, to make some trial of their dispositions.

SIR PETER. Ah! there needs no art to discover their merit — however, he shall have his way; but, pray, does he know
80 I am married?

ROWLEY. Yes, and will soon wish you joy.

SIR PETER. What, as we drink health to a friend in a consumption! Ah! Oliver will laugh at me. We used to rail at matrimony together, but he has been steady to his text. Well, he must be soon at my house, though — I'll instantly give orders for his reception. But, Master Rowley, don't drop a word that Lady Teazle and I ever disagree.

ROWLEY. By no means.

---

l.74 enjoin: *tell.*
l.77 dispositions: *characters.*

SIR PETER. For I should never be able to stand Noll's jokes; so I'll have him think, Lord forgive me! that we are a very 90 happy couple.

ROWLEY. I understand you: — but then you must be very careful not to differ while he is in the house with you.

SIR PETER. Egad, and so we must — and that's impossible. Ah, Master Rowley, when an old bachelor marries a young wife, he deserves — no — the crime carries its punishment along with it.   [Exeunt.

ACT II

SCENE I. *A Room in Sir Peter Teazle's House*
Enter SIR PETER *and* LADY TEAZLE

SIR PETER. Lady Teazle, Lady Teazle, I'll not bear it!

LADY TEAZLE. Sir Peter, Sir Peter, you may bear it or not, as you please; but I ought to have my own way in everything, and, what's more, I will too. What! though I was educated in the country, I know very well that women of fashion in London are accountable to nobody after they are married.

SIR PETER. Very well, ma'am, very well; so a husband is to have no influence, no authority?

LADY TEAZLE. Authority! No, to be sure: if you wanted 10 authority over me, you should have adopted me, and not married me: I am sure you were old enough.

SIR PETER. Old enough! — ay, there it is. Well, well, Lady Teazle, though my life may be made unhappy by your temper, I'll not be ruined by your extravagance!

LADY TEAZLE. My extravagance! I'm sure I'm not more extravagant than a woman of fashion ought to be.

SIR PETER. No, no, madam, you shall throw away no more sums on such unmeaning luxury. 'Slife! to spend as much

---

1.89 Noll: *Oliver.*

20   to furnish your dressing-room with flowers in winter as would suffice to turn the Pantheon into a greenhouse, and give a *fête champêtre* at Christmas.

LADY TEAZLE. And am I to blame, Sir Peter, because flowers are dear in cold weather? You should find fault with the climate, and not with me. For my part, I'm sure I wish it was spring all the year round, and that roses grew under our feet!

SIR PETER. Oons! madam — if you had been born to this, I shouldn't wonder at you talking thus; but you forget what
30   your situation was when I married you.

LADY TEAZLE. No, no, I don't; 'twas a very disagreeable one, or I should never have married you.

SIR PETER. Yes, yes, madam, you were then in somewhat a humbler style — the daughter of a plain country squire. Recollect, Lady Teazle, when I saw you first sitting at your tambour, in a pretty figured linen gown, with a bunch of keys at your side, your hair combed smooth over a roll, and your apartment hung round with fruits in worsted, of your own working.

40 LADY TEAZLE. Oh, yes! I remember it very well, and a curious life I led. My daily occupation to inspect the dairy, superintend the poultry, make extracts from the family receipt-book, and comb my aunt Deborah's lapdog.

SIR PETER. Yes, yes, ma'am, 'twas so indeed.

LADY TEAZLE. And then you know, my evening amusements! To draw patterns for ruffles, which I had not materials to make up; to play Pope Joan with the curate;

---

l.21 Pantheon: *a fashionable London concert hall of the day.*
l.22 fête champêtre: *an elaborate form of outdoor entertainment and picnic.*
l.36 tambour: *a frame for embroidery.*
l.37 roll: *a pad of hair; part of a lady's head-dress.*
l.43 receipt: *we would probably now say 'recipe'.*
l.46 ruffles: *a form of trimming.*
l.47 Pope Joan: *a card game.*

to read a sermon to my aunt; or to be stuck down to an old
spinet to strum my father to sleep after a fox-chase.

SIR PETER. I am glad you have so good a memory. Yes, 50
madam these were the recreations I took you from; but
now you must have your coach — *vis-à-vis* — and three
powdered footmen before your chair; and, in the summer,
a pair of white cats to draw you to Kensington Gardens.
No recollection, I suppose, when you were content to ride
double, behind the butler, on a docked coach-horse.

LADY TEAZLE. No — I swear I never did that: I deny the
butler and the coach-horse.

SIR PETER. This, madam, was your situation; and what have
I done for you? I have made you a woman of fashion, of 60
fortune, of rank — in short, I have made you my wife.

LADY TEAZLE. Well, then, and there is but one thing more
you can make me to add to the obligation, that is ——

SIR PETER. My widow, I suppose?

LADY TEAZLE. Hem! hem!

SIR PETER. I thank you, madam — but don't flatter yourself,
for though your ill conduct may disturb my peace of mind,
it shall never break my heart, I promise you: however, I
am equally obliged to you for the hint.

LADY TEAZLE. Then why will you endeavour to make your- 70
self so disagreeable to me, and thwart me in every little
elegant expense?

SIR PETER. 'Slife, madam, I say, had you any of these little
elegant expenses when you married me?

LADY TEAZLE. Lud, Sir Peter! would you have me be out of
the fashion?

---

l.49 spinet: *an instrument; the ancestor of the piano.*
l.52 vis-à-vis: *i.e. a coach in which the occupants sat facing one
another.*
l.53 chair: *Sedan-chair.*
l.54 Kensington Gardens: *then, as now, a fashionable London park.*

SIR PETER. The fashion, indeed! what had you to do with the fashion before you married me?

LADY TEAZLE. For my part, I should think you would like to
80 have your wife thought a woman of taste.

SIR PETER. Ay — there again — taste! Zounds! madam, you had no taste when you married me!

LADY TEAZLE. That's very true, indeed, Sir Peter! and, after having married you, I should never pretend to taste again, I allow. But now, Sir Peter, since we have finished our daily jangle, I presume I may go to my engagement at Lady Sneerwell's.

SIR PETER. Ay, there's another precious circumstance — a charming set of acquaintance you have made there!

90 LADY TEAZLE. Nay, Sir Peter, they are all people of rank and fortune, and remarkably tenacious of reputation.

SIR PETER. Yes, egad, they are tenacious of reputation with a vengeance; for they don't choose anybody should have a character but themselves! Such a crew! Ah! many a wretch has rid on a hurdle who has done less mischief than these utterers of forged tales, coiners of scandal, and clippers of reputation.

LADY TEAZLE. What, would you restrain the freedom of speech?

100 SIR PETER. Ah! they had made you just as bad as any one of the society.

LADY TEAZLE. Why, I believe I do bear a part with a tolerable grace.

SIR PETER. Grace indeed!

LADY TEAZLE. But I vow I bear no malice against the people I abuse: when I say an ill-natured thing, 'tis out of pure good humour; and I take it for granted they deal exactly

---

l.95 rid on a hurdle: *criminals were dragged to execution on hurdles.*
l.97 clippers: *it was the custom for dishonest people to clip the edges of coins and thus reduce their value.*

in the same manner with me. But, Sir Peter, you know you promised to come to Lady Sneerwell's too.

SIR PETER. Well, well, I'll call in, just to look after my own 110 character.

LADY TEAZLE. Then indeed, you must make haste after me, or you'll be too late. So good-bye to ye.   [*Exit.*

SIR PETER. So — I have gained much by my intended expostulation! Yet with what a charming air she contradicts every thing I say, and how pleasantly she shows her contempt for my authority! Well, though I can't make her love me, there is great satisfaction in quarrelling with her; and I think she never appears to such advantage as when she is doing every thing in her power to plague me.   120
                                             [*Exit.*

SCENE II. *A Room in Lady Sneerwell's House*

LADY SNEERWELL, MRS. CANDOUR, CRABTREE, SIR BENJAMIN BACKBITE, *and* JOSEPH SURFACE, *discovered*

LADY SNEERWELL. Nay, positively, we will hear it.

JOSEPH SURFACE. Yes, yes, the epigram, by all means.

SIR BENJAMIN. O plague on't, uncle! 'tis mere nonsense.

CRABTREE. No, no; 'fore Gad, very clever for an extempore!

SIR BENJAMIN. But, ladies, you should be acquainted with the circumstance. You must know, that one day last week, as Lady Betty Curricle was taking the dust in Hyde Park, in a sort of duodecimo phaeton, she desired me to write some verses on her ponies; upon which I took out my pocket-book, and in one moment produced the follow- 10 ing:—

---

l.7 Curricle: *a smart, fast form of carriage.*
l.8 duodecimo: *very small;* phaeton: *another popular type of carriage.*

Sure never were seen two such beautiful ponies;
Other horses are clowns, but these macaronies:
To give them this title I'm sure can't be wrong,
Their legs are so slim, and their tails are so long.

CRABTREE. There, ladies, done in the smack of a whip, and on horseback too.

JOSEPH SURFACE. A very Phœbus, mounted — indeed, Sir Benjamin!

20 SIR BENJAMIN. Oh dear, sir! trifles — trifles.

Enter LADY TEAZLE *and* MARIA

MRS. CANDOUR. I must have a copy.

LADY SNEERWELL. Lady Teazle, I hope we shall see Sir Peter?

LADY TEAZLE. I believe he'll wait on your ladyship presently.

LADY SNEERWELL. Maria, my love, you look grave. Come, you shall sit down to piquet with Mr. Surface.

MARIA. I take very little pleasure in cards — however, I'll do as your ladyship pleases.

30 LADY TEAZLE. [*Aside*]. I am surprised Mr. Surface should sit down with her; I thought he would have embraced this opportunity of speaking to me before Sir Peter came.

MRS. CANDOUR. Now, I'll die, but you are so scandalous, I'll forswear your society.

LADY TEAZLE. What's the matter, Mrs. Candour?

MRS. CANDOUR. They'll not allow our friend Miss Vermilion to be handsome.

LADY SNEERWELL. Oh, surely she is a pretty woman.

CRABTREE. I am very glad you think so, ma'am.

---

l.13 macaronies: *smart, somewhat overdressed and fashionable young men.*
l.18 Phœbus: *Phœbus Apollo, the sun god, embodied power and grace.*
l.27 piquet: *a card game.*

MRS. CANDOUR. She has a charming fresh colour.   40

LADY TEAZLE. Yes, when it is fresh put on.

MRS. CANDOUR. Oh, fie! I'll swear her colour is natural: I have seen it come and go!

LADY TEAZLE. I dare swear you have, ma'am: it goes off at night, and comes again in the morning.

SIR BENJAMIN. True, ma'am, it not only comes and goes; but, what's more, egad, her maid can fetch and carry it!

MRS. CANDOUR. Ha! ha! ha! how I hate to hear you talk so! But surely, now, her sister is, or was, very handsome.

CRABTREE. Who? Mrs. Evergreen? O Lord! she's six-and-   50 fifty if she's an hour!

MRS. CANDOUR. Now positively you wrong her; fifty-two or fifty-three is the utmost — and I don't think she looks more.

SIR BENJAMIN. Ah! there's no judging by her looks, unless one could see her face.

LADY SNEERWELL. Well, well, if Mrs. Evergreen does take some pains to repair the ravages of time, you must allow she effects it with great ingenuity; and surely that's better than the careless manner in which the widow Ochre   60 caulks her wrinkles.

SIR BENJAMIN. Nay, now, Lady Sneerwell, you are severe upon the widow. Come, come, 'tis not that she paints so ill — but, when she has finished her face, she joins it on so badly to her neck, that she looks like a mended statue, in which the connoisseur may see at once that the head is modern, though the trunk's antique.

CRABTREE. Ha! ha! ha! Well said, nephew!

MRS. CANDOUR. Ha! ha! ha! Well, you make me laugh; but I vow I hate you for it. What do you think of Miss   70 Simper?

1.61 caulks: *stops up; literally to stop up the leaks in a boat.*

SIR BENJAMIN. Why, she has very pretty teeth.

LADY TEAZLE. Yes; and on that account, when she is neither speaking nor laughing (which very seldom happens), she never absolutely shuts her mouth, but leaves it always a-jar, as it were — thus. [*Shows her teeth.*

MRS. CANDOUR. How can you be so ill-natured?

LADY TEAZLE. Nay, I allow even that's better than the pains Mrs. Prim takes to conceal her losses in front. She draws
80 her mouth till it positively resembles the aperture of a poor's-box, and all her words appear to slide out edgewise, as it were — thus: [*Mimics*] How do you do, madam? Yes, madam.

LADY SNEERWELL. Very well, Lady Teazle; I see you can be a little severe.

LADY TEAZLE. In defence of a friend it is but justice. But here comes Sir Peter to spoil our pleasantry.

Enter SIR PETER TEAZLE

SIR PETER. Ladies, your most obedient. — [*Aside.*] Mercy on me, here is the whole set! a character dead at every word,
90 I suppose.

MRS. CANDOUR. I am rejoiced you are come, Sir Peter. They have been so censorious — and Lady Teazle as bad as anyone.

SIR PETER. That must be very distressing to you, indeed, Mrs. Candour.

MRS. CANDOUR. Oh, they will allow good qualities to nobody; not even good nature to our friend Mrs. Pursy.

LADY TEAZLE. What, the fat dowager who was at Mrs. Quadrille's last night?

100 MRS. CANDOUR. Nay, her bulk is her misfortune; and, when she takes so much pains to get rid of it, you ought not to reflect on her.

---

l.81 poor's-box: *a box placed in a church for alms for the poor. It normally has a narrow slit for coins.*

LADY SNEERWELL. That's very true, indeed.

LADY TEAZLE. Yes, I know she almost lives on acids and small whey; laces herself by pulleys; and often, in the hottest noon in summer, you may see her on a little squat pony, with her hair plaited up behind like a drummer's and puffing round the Ring on a full trot.

MRS. CANDOUR. I thank you, Lady Teazle, for defending her.   110

SIR PETER. Yes, a good defence, truly.

MRS. CANDOUR. Truly, Lady Teazle is as censorious as Miss Sallow.

CRABTREE. Yes, and she is a curious being to pretend to be censorious — an awkward gawky, without any one good point under heaven.

MRS. CANDOUR. Positively you shall not be so very severe. Miss Sallow is a near relation of mine by marriage, and, as for her person, great allowance is to be made; for, let me tell you, a woman labours under many disadvantages who 120 tries to pass for a girl of six-and-thirty.

LADY SNEERWELL. Though, surely, she is handsome still — and for the weakness in her eyes, considering how much she reads by candlelight, it is not to be wondered at.

MRS. CANDOUR. True, and then as to her manner; upon my word I think it is particularly graceful, considering she never had the least education: for you know her mother was a Welsh milliner, and her father a sugar-baker at Bristol.

SIR BENJAMIN. Ah! you are both of you too good-natured! 130

SIR PETER. [Aside]. Yes, damned good-natured! This their own relation! mercy on me!

---

l.105 whey: *watery milk.*
l.108 the Ring: *a part of Hyde Park in London laid out for riding.*
l.128 sugar-baker: *sugar refiner.*

MRS. CANDOUR. For my part, I own I cannot bear to hear a friend ill-spoken of.

SIR PETER. No, to be sure!

SIR BENJAMIN. Oh! you are of a moral turn. Mrs. Candour and I can sit for an hour and hear Lady Stucco talk sentiment.

LADY TEAZLE. Nay, I vow Lady Stucco is very well with the
140   desert after dinner; for she's just like the French fruit one cracks for mottoes — made up of paint and proverb.

MRS. CANDOUR. Well, I will never join in ridiculing a friend; and so I constantly tell my cousin Ogle, and you all know what pretensions she has to be critical on beauty.

CRABTREE. Oh, to be sure! she has herself the oddest countenance that ever was seen; 'tis a collection of features from all the different countries of the globe.

SIR BENJAMIN. So she has, indeed — an Irish front ——

CRABTREE. Caledonian locks ——

150   SIR BENJAMIN. Dutch nose ——

CRABTREE. Austrian lips ——

SIR BENJAMIN. Complexion of a Spaniard ——

CRABTREE. And teeth *à la Chinoise* ——

SIR BENJAMIN. In short, her face resembles a *table d'hôte* at Spa — where no two guests are of a nation ——

CRABTREE. Or a congress at the close of a general war — wherein all the members, even to her eyes, appear to have a different interest, and her nose and chin are the only parties likely to join issue.

160   MRS. CANDOUR. Ha! ha! ha!

---

l.137 sentiment: *emotional subjects.*
l.154 table d'hôte: *a common table for guests at a hotel.*
l.155 Spa: *an inland resort usually having health-giving mineral springs, e.g. Bath, Cheltenham, Leamington.*

SIR PETER. [*Aside*]. Mercy on my life! — a person they dine with twice a week!

MRS. CANDOUR. Nay, but I vow you shall not carry the laugh off so — for give me leave to say, that Mrs. Ogle ——

SIR PETER. Madam, madam, I beg your pardon — there's no stopping these good gentlemen's tongues. But when I tell you, Mrs. Candour, that the lady they are abusing is a particular friend of mine, I hope you'll not take her part.

LADY SNEERWELL. Ha! ha! ha! well said, Sir Peter! but you are a cruel creature — too phlegmatic yourself for a jest, 170 and too peevish to allow wit in others.

SIR PETER. Ah, madam, true wit is more nearly allied to good nature than your ladyship is aware of.

LADY TEAZLE. True, Sir Peter: I believe they are so near akin that they can never be united.

SIR BENJAMIN. Or rather, suppose them man and wife, because one seldom sees them together.

LADY TEAZLE. But Sir Peter is such an enemy to scandal, I believe he would have it put down by Parliament.

SIR PETER. 'Fore heaven, madam, if they were to consider 180 the sporting with reputation of as much importance as poaching on manors, and pass an act for the preservation of fame, I believe many would thank them for the bill.

LADY SNEERWELL. O Lud! Sir Peter; would you deprive us of our privileges?

SIR PETER. Ay, madam; and then no person should be permitted to kill characters and run down reputations, but qualified old maids and disappointed widows.

LADY SNEERWELL. Go, you monster!

MRS. CANDOUR. But, surely, you would not be quite so 190 severe on those who only report what they hear?

SIR PETER. Yes, madam, I would have law merchant for

1.192 law merchant: *mercantile law.*

them too; and in all cases of slander currency, whenever the drawer of the lie was not to be found, the injured parties should have a right to come on any of the indorsers.

CRABTREE. Well, for my part, I believe there never was a scandalous tale without some foundation.

LADY SNEERWELL. Come, ladies, shall we sit down to cards in the next room?

Enter SERVANT, *who whispers to* SIR PETER

200 SIR PETER. [*Aside*]. I'll be with them directly. — [*Exit* SERVANT] I'll get away unperceived.

LADY SNEERWELL. Sir Peter, you are not going to leave us?

SIR PETER. Your ladyship must excuse me; I'm called away by particular business. But I leave my character behind me. [*Exit.*

SIR BENJAMIN. Well — certainly, Lady Teazle, that lord of yours is a strange being: I could tell you some stories of him would make you laugh heartily if he were not your husband.

210 LADY TEAZLE. Oh, pray don't mind that; come, do let's hear them.

[*Exeunt all but* JOSEPH SURFACE *and* MARIA

JOSEPH SURFACE. Maria, I see you have no satisfaction in this society.

MARIA. How is it possible I should? If to raise malicious smiles at the infirmities or misfortunes of those who have never injured us be the province of wit or humour, Heaven grant me a double portion of dullness!

JOSEPH SURFACE. Yet they appear more ill-natured than they are; they have no malice at heart.

l.193 slander currency: *slander circulating from one person to another.*
l.194 drawer: *one who draws up a deed promising to repay money.*
l.195 the indorsers: *those who guarantee a deed.*

MARIA. Then is their conduct still more contemptible; for, 220
in my opinion, nothing could excuse the intemperance of
their tongues but a natural and uncontrollable bitterness of
mind.

JOSEPH SURFACE. Undoubtedly, madam; and it has always
been a sentiment of mine, that to propagate a malicious
truth wantonly is more despicable than to falsify from
revenge. But can you, Maria, feel thus for others, and be
unkind to me alone? Is hope to be denied the tenderest
passion?

MARIA. Why will you distress me by renewing this subject? 230

JOSEPH SURFACE. Ah, Maria! you would not treat me thus,
and oppose your guardian, Sir Peter's will, but that I see
that profligate Charles is still a favoured rival.

MARIA. Ungenerously urged! But, whatever my sentiments
are for that unfortunate young man, be assured I shall not
feel more bound to give him up, because his distresses
have lost him the regard even of a brother.

JOSEPH SURFACE. Nay, but, Maria, do not leave me with a
frown: by all that's honest, I swear ——   [*Kneels.*

Re-enter LADY TEAZLE *behind*

[*Aside.*] Gad's life, here's Lady Teazle. — [*Aloud to* MARIA.] 240
You must not — no, you shall not — for, though I have the
greatest regard for Lady Teazle ——

MARIA. Lady Teazle!

JOSEPH SURFACE. Yet were Sir Peter to suspect ——

LADY TEAZLE. [*Coming forward*]. What is this, pray? Does he
take her for me? — Child, you are wanted in the next
room. — [*Exit* MARIA.] What is all this, pray?

JOSEPH SURFACE. Oh, the most unlucky circumstance in
nature! Maria has somehow suspected the tender concern
I have for your happiness, and threatened to acquaint Sir 250

---

l.225 sentiment: *opinion.*

Peter with her suspicions, and I was just endeavouring to reason with her when you came in.

LADY TEAZLE. Indeed! but you seemed to adopt a very tender mode of reasoning — do you usually argue on your knees?

JOSEPH SURFACE. Oh, she's a child, and I thought a little bombast —— But, Lady Teazle, when are you to give me your judgment on my library, as you promised?

LADY TEAZLE. No, no; I begin to think it would be impru-
260   dent, and you know I admit you as a lover no farther than fashion requires.

JOSEPH SURFACE. True — a mere Platonic cicisbeo, what every wife is entitled to.

LADY TEAZLE. Certainly, one must not be out of the fashion. However, I have so many of my country prejudices left, that, though Sir Peter's ill humour may vex me ever so, it never shall provoke me to ——

JOSEPH SURFACE. The only revenge in your power. Well, I applaud your moderation.

270 LADY TEAZLE. Go — you are an insinuating wretch! But we shall be missed — let us join the company.

JOSEPH SURFACE. But we had best not return together.

LADY TEAZLE. Well, don't stay; for Maria sha'n't come to hear any more of your reasoning, I promise you.   [Exit.

JOSEPH SURFACE. A curious dilemma, truly, my politics have run me into! I wanted, at first, only to ingratiate myself with Lady Teazle, that she might not be my enemy with Maria; and I have, I don't know how, become her serious lover. Sincerely I begin to wish I had never made such a
280   point of gaining so very good a character, for it has led me

l.262 Platonic cicisbeo: *'friend of the family'*; cicisbeo *is an Italian term for the admirer of a married woman.*
l.275 politics: *schemes.*

into so many cursed rogueries that I doubt I shall be
exposed at last.   [*Exit.*

SCENE III. *A Room in Sir Peter Teazle's House*
Enter SIR OLIVER SURFACE *and* ROWLEY

SIR OLIVER. Ha! ha! ha! so my old friend is married, hey?
— a young wife out of the country. Ha! ha! ha! that he
should have stood bluff to old bachelor so long, and sink
into a husband at last!

ROWLEY. But you must not rally him on the subject, Sir
Oliver; 'tis a tender point, I assure you, though he has
been married only seven months.

SIR OLIVER. Then he has been just half a year on the stool of
repentance! — Poor Peter! But you say he has entirely
given up Charles — never sees him, hey?   10

ROWLEY. His prejudice against him is astonishing, and I am
sure greatly increased by a jealousy of him with Lady
Teazle, which he has industriously been led into by a scandalous society in the neighbourhood, who have contri-
buted not a little to Charles's ill name. Whereas the truth
is, I believe, if the lady is partial to either of them, his
brother is the favourite.

SIR OLIVER. Ay, I know there are a set of malicious, prating,
prudent gossips, both male and female, who murder
characters to kill time, and will rob a young fellow of his   20
good name before he has years to know the value of it. But
I am not to be prejudiced against my nephew by such, I
promise you! No, no: if Charles has done nothing false or
mean, I shall compound for his extravagance.

ROWLEY. Then, my life on't, you will reclaim him. Ah, sir,
it gives me new life to find that your heart is not turned
against him, and that the son of my good old master has
one friend, however, left.

---

l.281 I doubt: *I am sure.*
l.24 compound for: *compromise over.*

SIR OLIVER. What! shall I forget, Master Rowley, when I
was at his years myself? Egad, my brother and I were
neither of us very prudent youths; and yet, I believe, you
have not seen many better men than your old master was?

ROWLEY. Sir, 'tis this reflection gives me assurance that
Charles may yet be a credit to his family. But here comes
Sir Peter.

SIR OLIVER. Egad, so he does! Mercy on me! he's greatly
altered, and seems to have a settled married look! One
may read husband in his face at this distance!

Enter SIR PETER TEAZLE

SIR PETER. Ha! Sir Oliver — my old friend! Welcome to
England a thousand times!

SIR OLIVER. Thank you, thank you, Sir Peter! and i' faith
I am glad to find you well, believe me!

SIR PETER. Oh! 'tis a long time since we met — fifteen years,
I doubt, Sir Oliver, and many a cross accident in the
time.

SIR OLIVER. Ay, I have had my share. But, what! I find you
are married, hey, my old boy? Well, well, it can't be
helped; and so — I wish you joy with all my heart!

SIR PETER. Thank you, thank you, Sir Oliver. — Yes, I have
entered into — the happy state; but we'll not talk of that
now.

SIR OLIVER. True, true, Sir Peter; old friends should not
begin on grievances at first meeting. No, no, no.

ROWLEY. [*Aside to* SIR OLIVER]. Take care, pray, sir.

SIR OLIVER. Well, so one of my nephews is a wild rogue,
hey?

SIR PETER. Wild! Ah! my old friend, I grieve for your
disappointment there; he's a lost young man, indeed.
However, his brother will make you amends; Joseph is,

---

l.44 cross: *adverse.*

indeed, what a youth should be — everybody in the world 60 speaks well of him.

SIR OLIVER. I am sorry to hear it; he has too good a character to be an honest fellow. Everybody speaks well of him! Pshaw! then he has bowed as low to knaves and fools as to the honest dignity of genius and virtue.

SIR PETER. What, Sir Oliver! do you blame him for not making enemies?

SIR OLIVER. Yes, if he has merit enough to deserve them.

SIR PETER. Well, well — you'll be convinced when you know him. 'Tis edification to hear him converse; he pro- 70 fesses the noblest sentiments.

SIR OLIVER. Oh, plague of his sentiments! If he salutes me with a scrap of morality in his mouth, I shall be sick directly. But, however, don't mistake me, Sir Peter; I don't mean to defend Charles's errors: but, before I form my judgment of either of them, I intend to make a trial of their hearts; and my friend Rowley and I have planned something for the purpose.

ROWLEY. And Sir Peter shall own for once he has been mistaken.   80

SIR PETER. Oh, my life on Joseph's honour!

SIR OLIVER. Well — come, give us a bottle of good wine, and we'll drink the lads' health, and tell you our scheme.

SIR PETER. *Allons*, then!

SIR OLIVER. And don't, Sir Peter, be so severe against your old friend's son. Odds my life! I am not sorry that he has run out of the course a little: for my part, I hate to see prudence clinging to the green suckers of youth; 'tis like ivy round a sapling, and spoils the growth of the tree.

                                                                                   [*Exeunt.*

---

l.84 Allons: *Come!*

ACT III

Scene I. *A Room in Sir Peter Teazle's House*

Enter SIR PETER TEAZLE, SIR OLIVER SURFACE, *and* ROWLEY

SIR PETER. Well, then, we will see this fellow first, and have our wine afterwards. But how is this, Master Rowley? I don't see the jest of your scheme.

ROWLEY. Why, sir, this Mr. Stanley, whom I was speaking of, is nearly related to them by their mother. He was once a merchant in Dublin, but has been ruined by a series of undeserved misfortunes. He has applied, by letter, since his confinement, both to Mr. Surface and Charles: from the former he has received nothing but evasive promises
10 of future service, while Charles has done all that his extravagance has left him power to do; and he is, at this time, endeavouring to raise a sum of money, part of which, in the midst of his own distresses, I know he intends for the service of poor Stanley.

SIR OLIVER. Ah! he is my brother's son.

SIR PETER. Well, but how is Sir Oliver personally to ——

ROWLEY. Why, sir, I will inform Charles and his brother that Stanley has obtained permission to apply personally to his friends; and, as they have neither of them ever seen
20 him, let Sir Oliver assume his character, and he will have a fair opportunity of judging, at least, of the benevolence of their dispositions: and believe me, sir, you will find in the youngest brother one who, in the midst of folly and dissipation, has still, as our immortal bard expresses it, — 'a hearty to pity, and a hand, open as day, for melting charity.'

---

l.3 jest: *point.*
l.24 our immortal bard: *i.e. Shakespeare. The quotation is from* 2 Henry *IV. iv.* 31, 32.

SIR PETER. Pshaw! What signifies his having an open hand or purse either, when he has nothing left to give? Well, well, make the trial, if you please. But where is the fellow whom you brought for Sir Oliver to examine, relative to 30 Charles's affairs?

ROWLEY. Below, waiting his commands, and no one can give him better intelligence. — This, Sir Oliver, is a friendly Jew, who, to do him justice, has done everything in his power to bring your nephew to a proper sense of his extravagance.

SIR PETER. Pray let us have him in.

ROWLEY. [*Calls to* SERVANT]. Desire Mr. Moses to walk up stairs.

SIR PETER. But, pray, why should you suppose he will 40 speak the truth?

ROWLEY. Oh, I have convinced him that he has no chance of recovering certain sums advanced to Charles but through the bounty of Sir Oliver, who he knows is arrived; so that you may depend on his fidelity to his own interests. I have also another evidence in my power, one Snake, whom I have detected in a matter little short of forgery, and shall shortly produce to remove some of your prejudices, Sir Peter, relative to Charles and Lady Teazle.

SIR PETER. I have heard too much on that subject.   50

ROWLEY. Here comes the honest Israelite.

Enter MOSES

— This is Sir Oliver.

SIR OLIVER. Sir, I understand you have lately had great dealings with my nephew Charles.

MOSES. Yes, Sir Oliver, I have done all I could for him; but he was ruined before he came to me for assistance.

SIR OLIVER. That was unlucky, truly; for you have had no opportunity of showing your talents.

MOSES. None at all; I hadn't the pleasure of knowing his
60 distresses till he was some thousands worse than nothing.

SIR OLIVER. Unfortunate, indeed! But I suppose you have
done all in your power for him, honest Moses?

MOSES. Yes, he knows that. This very evening I was to have
brought him a gentleman from the city, who does not
know him, and will, I believe, advance him some money.

SIR PETER. What, one Charles has never had money from
before?

MOSES. Yes, Mr. Premium, of Crutched Friars, formerly a
broker.

70 SIR PETER. Egad, Sir Oliver, a thought strikes me! —
Charles, you say, does not know Mr. Premium?

MOSES. Not at all.

SIR PETER. Now then, Sir Oliver, you may have a better
opportunity of satisfying yourself than by an old romancing
tale of a poor relation: go with my friend Moses, and
represent Premium, and then, I'll answer for it, you'll see
your nephew in all his glory.

SIR OLIVER. Egad, I like this idea better than the other,
and I may visit Joseph afterwards as old Stanley.

80 SIR PETER. True — so you may.

ROWLEY. Well, this is taking Charles rather at a disadvan-
tage, to be sure. However, Moses, you understand Sir
Peter, and will be faithful?

MOSES. You may depend upon me. [*Looks at his watch.*]
This is near the time I was to have gone.

SIR OLIVER. I'll accompany you as soon as you please,
Moses —— But hold! I have forgot one thing — how the
plague shall I be able to pass for a Jew?

MOSES. There's no need — the principal is Christian.

---

l.68 Crutched Friars: *a street in the City of London.*
l.89 principal: *the man who advanced the money.*

SIR OLIVER. Is he? I'm very sorry to hear it. But, then 90 again, an't I rather too smartly dressed to look like a money lender?

SIR PETER. Not at all; 'twould not be out of character, if you went in your own carriage — would it, Moses?

MOSES. Not in the least.

SIR OLIVER. Well, but how must I talk; there's certainly some cant of usury and mode of treating that I ought to know.

SIR PETER. Oh, there's not much to learn. The great point, as I take it, is to be exorbitant enough in your demands. 100 Hey, Moses?

MOSES. Yes, that's a very great point.

SIR OLIVER. I'll answer for't I'll not be wanting in that. I'll ask him eight or ten per cent. on the loan, at least.

MOSES. If you ask him no more than that, you'll be discovered immediately.

SIR OLIVER. Hey! what, the plague! how much then?

MOSES. That depends upon the circumstances. If he appears not very anxious for the supply, you should require only forty or fifty per cent.; but if you find him in great dis- 110 tress, and want the moneys very bad, you may ask double.

SIR PETER. A good honest trade you're learning, Sir Oliver!

SIR OLIVER. Truly, I think so — and not unprofitable.

MOSES. Then, you know, you haven't the moneys yourself, but are forced to borrow them for him of a friend.

SIR OLIVER. Oh! I borrow it of a friend, do I?

MOSES. And your friend is an unconscionable dog: but you can't help that.

SIR OLIVER. My friend an unconscionable dog, is he?

MOSES. Yes, and he himself has not the moneys by him, but 120 is forced to sell stock at a great loss.

SIR OLIVER. He is forced to sell stock at a great loss, is he? Well, that's very kind of him.

SIR PETER. I' faith, Sir Oliver — Mr. Premium, I mean — you'll soon be master of the trade. But, Moses! would not you have him run out a little against the Annuity Bill? That would be in character, I should think.

MOSES. Very much.

ROWLEY. And lament that a young man now must be at
130   years of discretion before he is suffered to ruin himself?

MOSES. Ay, great pity!

SIR PETER. And abuse the public for allowing merit to an act whose only object is to snatch misfortune and imprudence from the rapacious gripe of usury, and give the minor a chance of inheriting his estate without being undone by coming into possession.

SIR OLIVER. So, so — Moses shall give me farther instruction as we go together.

SIR PETER. You will not have much time, for your nephew
140   lives hard by.

SIR OLIVER. Oh, never fear! my tutor appears so able, that though Charles lived in the next street, it must be my own fault if I am not a complete rogue before I turn the corner.
                                                    [*Exit with* MOSES.

SIR PETER. So, now, I think Sir Oliver will be convinced: you are partial, Rowley, and would have prepared Charles for the other plot.

ROWLEY. No, upon my word, Sir Peter.

SIR PETER. Well, go bring me this Snake, and I'll hear what
150   he has to say presently. I see Maria, and want to speak with her. [*Exit* ROWLEY.] I should be glad to be convinced my suspicions of Lady Teazle and Charles were

---

l.126 Annuity Bill: *a Bill passed in* 1777 *making void all contracts for annuities made with people under* 21.
l.140 hard by: *near here.*

unjust. I have never yet opened my mind on this subject to my friend Joseph — I am determined I will do it — he will give me his opinion sincerely.

Enter MARIA

So, child, has Mr. Surface returned with you?

MARIA. No, sir; he was engaged.

SIR PETER. Well, Maria, do you not reflect, the more you converse with that amiable young man, what return his partiality for you deserves?   160

MARIA. Indeed, Sir Peter, your frequent importunity on this subject distresses me extremely — you compel me to declare, that I know no man who has ever paid me a particular attention whom I would not prefer to Mr. Surface.

SIR PETER. So — here's perverseness! No, no, Maria, 'tis Charles only whom you would prefer. 'Tis evident his vices and follies have won your heart.

MARIA. This is unkind, sir. You know I have obeyed you in neither seeing nor corresponding with him: I have heard enough to convince me that he is unworthy my regard. Yet 170 I cannot think it culpable, if, while my understanding severely condemns his vices, my heart suggests some pity for his distresses.

SIR PETER. Well, well, pity him as much as you please; but give your heart and hand to a worthier object.

MARIA. Never to his brother!

SIR PETER. Go, perverse and obstinate! But take care, madam; you have never yet known what the authority of a guardian is: don't compel me to inform you of it.

MARIA. I can only say, you shall not have just reason. 'Tis 180 true, by my father's will, I am for a short period bound to regard you as his substitute; but must cease to think you so, when you would compel me to be miserable.   [*Exit.*

SIR PETER. Was ever man so crossed as I am, everything conspiring to fret me! I had not been involved in matrimony a fortnight, before her father, a hale and hearty man, died, on purpose, I believe, for the pleasure of plaguing me with the care of his daughter. — [LADY TEAZLE *sings without.*] But here comes my helpmate! She appears in great good humour. How happy I should be if I could tease her into loving me, though but a little!

Enter LADY TEAZLE

LADY TEAZLE. Lud! Sir Peter, I hope you haven't been quarrelling with Maria? It is not using me well to be ill-humoured when I am not by.

SIR PETER. Ah, Lady Teazle, you might have the power to make me good-humoured at all times.

LADY TEAZLE. I am sure I wish I had; for I want you to be in a charming sweet temper at this moment. Do be good-humoured now, and let me have two hundred pounds, will you?

SIR PETER. Two hundred pounds; what, an't I to be in a good humour without paying for it! But speak to me thus, and i' faith there's nothing I could refuse you. You shall have it; but seal me a bond for the repayment.

LADY TEAZLE. Oh, no — there — my note of hand will do as well.   [*Offering her hand.*

SIR PETER. And you shall no longer reproach me with not giving you an independent settlement. I mean shortly to surprise you: but shall we always live thus, hey?

LADY TEAZLE. If you please. I'm sure I don't care how soon we leave off quarrelling, provided you'll own you were tired first.

SIR PETER. Well — then let our future contest, be who shall be most obliging.

LADY TEAZLE. I assure you, Sir Peter, good nature becomes you. You look now as you did before we were married, when you used to walk with me under the elms, and tell

me stories of what a gallant you were in your youth, and
chuck me under the chin, you would; and asked me if I
thought I could love an old fellow, who would deny me 220
nothing — didn't you?

SIR PETER. Yes, yes, and you were as kind and attentive ——

LADY TEAZLE. Ay, so I was, and would always take your
part, when my acquaintance used to abuse you, and turn
you into ridicule.

SIR PETER. Indeed!

LADY TEAZLE. Ay, and when my cousin Sophy has called
you a stiff, peevish old bachelor, and laughed at me for
thinking of marrying one who might be my father, I have
always defended you, and said, I didn't think you so ugly 230
by any means.

SIR PETER. Thank you.

LADY TEAZLE. And I dared say you'd make a very good sort
of a husband.

SIR PETER. And you prophesied right; and we shall now be
the happiest couple ——

LADY TEAZLE. And never differ again?

SIR PETER. No, never! — though at the same time, indeed,
my dear Lady Teazle, you must watch your temper very
seriously; for in all our little quarrels, my dear, if you 240
recollect, my love, you always began first.

LADY TEAZLE. I beg your pardon, my dear Sir Peter:
indeed, you always gave the provocation.

SIR PETER. Now see, my angel! take care — contradicting
isn't the way to keep friends.

LADY TEAZLE. Then don't you begin it, my love!

SIR PETER. There, now! you — you are going on. You don't
perceive, my life, that you are just doing the very thing
which you know always makes me angry.

LADY TEAZLE. Nay, you know, if you will be angry without 250
any reason, my dear ——

SIR PETER. There! now you want to quarrel again.

LADY TEAZLE. No, I'm sure I don't: but, if you will be so peevish ——

SIR PETER. There now! who begins first?

LADY TEAZLE. Why, you, to be sure. I said nothing — but there's no bearing your temper.

SIR PETER. No, no, madam: the fault's in your own temper.

LADY TEAZLE. Ay, you are just what my cousin Sophy said you would be.

SIR PETER. Your cousin Sophy is a forward, impertinent gipsy.

LADY TEAZLE. You are a great bear, I'm sure, to abuse my relations.

SIR PETER. Now may all the plagues of marriage be doubled on me, if ever I try to be friends with you any more!

LADY TEAZLE. So much the better.

SIR PETER. No, no, madam: 'tis evident you never cared a pin for me, and I was a madman to marry you — a pert, rural coquette, that had refused half the honest squires in the neighbourhood!

LADY TEAZLE. And I am sure I was a fool to marry you — an old dangling bachelor, who was single at fifty, only because he never could meet with anyone who would have him.

SIR PETER. Ay, ay, madam; but you were pleased enough to listen to me: you never had such an offer before.

LADY TEAZLE. No! didn't I refuse Sir Tivy Terrier, who everybody said would have been a better match? for his estate is just as good as yours, and he has broke his neck since we have been married.

SIR PETER. I have done with you, madam! You are an unfeeling, ungrateful — but there's an end of everything. I believe you capable of everything that is bad. Yes, madam, I now believe the reports relative to you and Charles, madam. Yes, madam, you and Charles are, not without grounds ——

LADY TEAZLE. Take care, Sir Peter! you had better not insinuate any such thing! I'll not be suspected without cause, I promise you.

SIR PETER. Very well, madam! very well! A separate maintenance as soon as you please. Yes, madam, or a divorce! I'll make an example of myself for the benefit of all old bachelors. Let us separate, madam.

LADY TEAZLE. Agreed! agreed! And now, my dear Sir Peter, we are of a mind once more, we may be the happiest couple, and never differ again, you know: ha! ha! ha! Well, you are going to be in a passion, I see, and I shall only interrupt you — so, bye! bye!

[*Exit.*

SIR PETER. Plagues and tortures! can't I make her angry either! Oh, I am the most miserable fellow! But I'll not bear her presuming to keep her temper: no! she may break my heart, but she sha'n't keep her temper.

[*Exit.*

SCENE II. *A Room in Charles Surface's House*

Enter TRIP, MOSES, *and* SIR OLIVER SURFACE

TRIP. Here, Master Moses! if you'll stay a moment I'll try whether — what's the gentleman's name?

SIR OLIVER. [*Aside to* MOSES]. Mr. Moses, what is my name?

MOSES. Mr. Premium.

TRIP. Premium — very well.   [*Exit, taking snuff.*

SIR OLIVER. To judge by the servants, one wouldn't believe the master was ruined. But what! — sure, this was my brother's house?

MOSES. Yes, sir; Mr. Charles bought it of Mr. Joseph, with the furniture, pictures, etc., just as the old gentleman left it. Sir Peter thought it a piece of extravagance in him.

SIR OLIVER. In my mind, the other's economy in selling it to him was more reprehensible by half.

Re-enter TRIP

TRIP. My master says you must wait, gentlemen: he has company, and can't speak with you yet.

SIR OLIVER. If he knew who it was wanted to see him, perhaps he would not send such a message.

TRIP. Yes, yes, sir; he knows you are here — I did not forget
20   little Premium: no, no, no.

SIR OLIVER. Very well; and I pray, sir, what may be your name?

TRIP. Trip, sir; my name is Trip, at your service.

SIR OLIVER. Well, then, Mr. Trip, you have a pleasant sort of place here, I guess?

TRIP. Why, yes — here are three or four of us pass our time agreeably enough; but then our wages are sometimes a little in arrear — and not very great either — but fifty pounds a year, and find our own bags and bouquets.

30 SIR OLIVER. [*Aside*]. Bags and bouquets! halters and bastinadoes!

TRIP. And *à propos*, Moses, have you been able to get me that little bill discounted?

SIR OLIVER. [*Aside*]. Wants to raise money too! — mercy on me! Has his distresses too, I warrant, like a lord, and affects creditors and duns.

MOSES. 'Twas not to be done, indeed, Mr. Trip.

---

l.29 bags: *pouches in which the back hair of the wig was curled;* bouquets: *finery.*
l.30 bastinadoes: *a form of punishment in which the victim is beaten on the soles of the feet.*
l.33 discounted bill: *a signed document promising the payment of money on the security of which a sum of money is lent.*
l.36 duns: *particularly urgent creditors.*

TRIP. Good lack, you surprise me! My friend Brush has
  indorsed it, and I thought when he put his name at the
  back of a bill 'twas the same as cash.   40

MOSES. No, 'twouldn't do.

TRIP. A small sum — but twenty pounds. Hark'ee, Moses,
  do you think you couldn't get it me by way of annuity?

SIR OLIVER. [Aside]. An annuity! ha! ha! a footman raise
  money by way of annuity! Well done, luxury, egad!

MOSES. Well, but you must insure your place.

TRIP. Oh, with all my heart! I'll insure my place, and my
  life too, if you please.

SIR OLIVER. [Aside]. It's more than I would your neck.

MOSES. But is there nothing you could deposit?   50

TRIP. Why, nothing capital of my master's wardrobe has
  dropped lately; but I could give you a mortgage on some
  of his winter clothes, with equity of redemption before
  November — or you shall have the reversion of the French
  velvet, or a post-obit on the blue and silver; — these, I
  should think, Moses, with a few pair of point ruffles, as a
  collateral security — hey, my little fellow?

MOSES. Well, well.   [Bell rings.

TRIP. Egad, I heard the bell! I believe, gentlemen, I can
  now introduce you. Don't forget the annuity, little Moses! 60
  This way, gentlemen. I'll insure my place, you know.

SIR OLIVER. [Aside]. If the man be a shadow of the master,
  this is the temple of dissipation indeed!   [Exeunt.

---

ll.51-2 nothing capital ... dropped lately: *i.e. I have had nothing
valuable from his wardrobe lately upon which I could borrow money.*
l.52 mortgage: *a particular form of loan.*
l.55 post-obit: *an agreement to repay a loan upon the death of some
person from whom the borrower has expectations.*
l.57 collateral security: *additional security.*

SCENE III. *Another Room in the same*

CHARLES SURFACE, SIR HARRY BUMPER, CARELESS,
and GENTLEMEN, *discovered drinking*

CHARLES SURFACE. 'Fore heaven, 'tis true! — there's the great degeneracy of the age. Many of our acquaintance have taste, spirit, and politeness; but, plague on't, they won't drink.

CARELESS. It is so, indeed, Charles! they give in to all the substantial luxuries of the table, and abstain from nothing but wine and wit. Oh, certainly society suffers by it intolerably! for now, instead of the social spirit of raillery that used to mantle over a glass of bright Burgundy, their 10 conversation is become just like the Spa-water they drink, which has all the pertness and flatulency of champagne, without its spirit or flavour.

FIRST GENTLEMAN. But what are they to do who love play better than wine?

CARELESS. True! there's Sir Harry diets himself for gaming, and is now under a hazard regimen.

CHARLES SURFACE. Then he'll have the worst of it. What! you wouldn't train a horse for the course by keeping him from corn? For my part, egad, I am never so successful as 20 when I am a little merry: let me throw on a bottle of champagne and I never lose.

ALL. Hey, what?

CHARLES SURFACE. At least I never feel my losses, which is exactly the same thing.

SECOND GENTLEMAN. Ay, that I believe.

CHARLES SURFACE. And then, what man can pretend to be a believer in love, who is an abjurer of wine? 'Tis the test by which the lover knows his own heart. Fill a dozen

---

1.16 a hazard regimen: *dieting himself in order to excel at hazard* (*a fashionable game of dice*).

bumpers to a dozen beauties, and she that floats at the top
is the maid that has bewitched you.   30

CARELESS. Now then, Charles, be honest, and give us your
real favourite.

CHARLES SURFACE. Why, I have withheld her only in compassion to you. If I toast her, you must give a round of her
peers, which is impossible — on earth.

CARELESS. Oh! then we'll find some canonised vestals or
heathen goddesses that will do, I warrant!

CHARLES SURFACE. Here then, bumpers, you rogues!
bumpers! Maria! Maria! ——

SIR HARRY. Maria who?   40

CHARLES SURFACE. Oh, damn the surname! — 'tis too formal
to be registered in Love's calendar — Maria!

ALL. Maria!

CHARLES SURFACE. But now, Sir Harry, beware, we must
have beauty superlative.

CARELESS. Nay, never study, Sir Harry: we'll stand to the
toast, though your mistress should want an eye, and you
know you have a song will excuse you.

SIR HARRY. Egad, so I have! and I'll give him the song
instead of the lady.   [*Sings.* 50

Here's to the maiden of bashful fifteen;
    Here's to the widow of fifty;
Here's to the flaunting extravagant quean,
    And here's to the housewife that's thrifty.

Chorus. Let the toast pass, —
        Drink to the lass,
I'll warrant she'll prove an excuse for the glass.

---

l.29 bumpers: *big glasses.*
l.35 peers: *equals.*
l.36 canonised vestals: *saintly women of unblemished reputation.*
l.53 quean: *woman.*

Here's to the charmer whose dimples we prize;
Now to the maid who has none, sir:
60   Here's to the girl with a pair of blue eyes,
And here's to the nymph with but one, sir.

Chorus.   Let the toast pass, etc.

Here's to the maid with a bosom of snow:
Now to her that's as brown as a berry:
Here's to the wife with a face full of woe,
And now to the damsel that's merry.

Chorus.   Let the toast pass, etc.

For let 'em be clumsy, or let 'em be slim,
Young or ancient, I care not a feather;
70   So fill a pint bumper quite up to the brim,
So fill up your glasses, nay, fill to the brim,
And let us e'en toast them together.

Chorus.   Let the toast pass, etc.

ALL. Bravo! bravo!

Enter TRIP, *and whispers to* CHARLES SURFACE

CHARLES SURFACE. Gentlemen, you must excuse me a little.
— Careless, take the chair, will you?

CARELESS. Nay, pr'ythee, Charles, what now? This is one
of your peerless beauties, I suppose, has dropped in by
chance?

80 CHARLES SURFACE. No, faith! To tell you the truth 'tis a
Jew and a broker, who are come by appointment.

CARELESS. Oh! let's have the Jew in.

FIRST GENTLEMAN. Ay, and the broker too, by all means.

SECOND GENTLEMAN. Yes, yes, the Jew and the broker.

CHARLES SURFACE. Egad, with all my heart! — Trip, bid
the gentlemen walk in. — [*Exit* TRIP.] Though there's
one of them a stranger, I can tell you.

CARELESS. Charles, let us give them some generous Burgundy, and perhaps they'll grow conscientious.

CHARLES SURFACE. Oh, hang 'em, no! wine does but draw 90 forth a man's natural qualities; and to make them drink would only be to whet their knavery.

Re-enter TRIP, *with* SIR OLIVER SURFACE *and* MOSES

CHARLES SURFACE. So, honest Moses; walk in, pray, Mr. Premium — that's the gentleman's name, isn't it, Moses?

MOSES. Yes, sir.

CHARLES SURFACE. Set chairs, Trip. — Sit down, Mr. Premium. — Glasses, Trip. — [TRIP *gives chairs and glasses, and exit.*] Sit down, Moses. — Come, Mr. Premium, I'll give you a sentiment; here's *Success to usury!* — Moses, fill the gentleman a bumper. 100

MOSES. Success to usury!   [*Drinks.*

CARELESS. Right, Moses — usury is prudence and industry, and deserves to succeed.

SIR OLIVER. Then here's — All the success it deserves!
                                                                 [*Drinks.*

CARELESS. No, no, that won't do! Mr. Premium, you have demurred at the toast, and must drink it in a pint bumper.

FIRST GENTLEMAN. A pint bumper, at least.

MOSES. Oh, pray, sir, consider — Mr. Premium's a gentleman.

CARELESS. And therefore loves good wine. 110

SECOND GENTLEMAN. Give Moses a quart glass — this is mutiny, and a high contempt for the chair.

CARELESS. Here, now for't! I'll see justice done to the last drop of the bottle.

SIR OLIVER. Nay, pray, gentlemen — I did not expect this usage.

---

l.99 sentiment: *toast.*

CHARLES SURFACE. No, hang it, you shan't; Mr. Premium's a stranger.

SIR OLIVER. [*Aside*]. Odd! I wish I was well out of their
120 company.

CARELESS. Plague on 'em then! if they won't drink, we'll not sit down with them. Come, Harry, the dice are in the next room. — Charles, you'll join us when you have finished your business with the gentlemen?

CHARLES SURFACE. I will! I will! — [*Exeunt* SIR HARRY BUMPER *and* GENTLEMEN; CARELESS *following*.] Careless!

CARELESS. [*returning*]. Well!

CHARLES SURFACE. Perhaps I may want you.

CARELESS. Oh, you know I am always ready: word, note, or
130 bond, 'tis all the same to me.   [*Exit.*

MOSES. Sir, this is Mr. Premium, a gentleman of the strictest honour and secrecy; and always performs what he undertakes. Mr. Premium, this is ——

CHARLES SURFACE. Pshaw! have done. Sir, my friend Moses is a very honest fellow, but a little slow at expression: he'll be an hour giving us our titles. Mr. Premium, the plain state of the matter is this: I am an extravagant young fellow who wants to borrow money; you I take to be a prudent old fellow, who has got money to lend. I am block-
140 head enough to give fifty per cent. sooner than not have it; and you, I presume, are rogue enough to take a hundred if you can get it. Now, sir, you see we are acquainted at once, and may proceed to business without farther ceremony.

SIR OLIVER. Exceeding frank, upon my word. I see, sir, you are not a man of many compliments.

CHARLES SURFACE. Oh, no, sir! plain dealing in business I always think best.

SIR OLIVER. Sir, I like you the better for it. However, you are mistaken in one thing; I have no money to lend, but I
150 believe I could procure some of a friend; but then he's an

unconscionable dog. Isn't he, Moses? And must sell stock to accommodate you. Mustn't he, Moses?

MOSES. Yes, indeed! You know I always speak the truth, and scorn to tell a lie!

CHARLES SURFACE. Right. People that speak truth generally do. But these are trifles, Mr. Premium. What! I know money isn't to be bought without paying for 't!

SIR OLIVER. Well, but what security could you give? You have no land, I suppose?

CHARLES SURFACE. Not a mole-hill, nor a twig, but what's in 160 the bough-pots out of the window!

SIR OLIVER. Nor any stock, I presume?

CHARLES SURFACE. Nothing but live stock — and that's only a few pointers and ponies. But pray, Mr. Premium, are you acquainted at all with any of my connections?

SIR OLIVER. Why, to say truth, I am.

CHARLES SURFACE. Then you must know that I have a devilish rich uncle in the East Indies, Sir Oliver Surface, from whom I have the greatest expectations?

SIR OLIVER. That you have a wealthy uncle, I have heard; 170 but how your expectations will turn out is more, I believe, than you can tell.

CHARLES SURFACE. Oh, no! — there can be no doubt. They tell me I'm a prodigious favourite, and that he talks of leaving me everything.

SIR OLIVER. Indeed! this is the first time I've heard of it.

CHARLES SURFACE. Yes, yes, 'tis just so. Moses knows 'tis true; don't you, Moses?

MOSES. Oh, yes! I'll swear to 't.

SIR OLIVER. [Aside]. Egad, they'll persuade me presently I'm 180 at Bengal.

---

l.161 the bough-pots: *pots for holding ornamental flowers or boughs.*
l.164 pointers: *a breed of sporting dog.*

CHARLES SURFACE. Now I propose, Mr. Premium, if it's
agreeable to you, a post-obit on Sir Oliver's life: though at
the same time the old fellow has been so liberal to me, that
I give you my word, I should be very sorry to hear that
anything had happened to him.

SIR OLIVER. Not more than I should, I assure you. But the
bond you mention happens to be just the worst security
you could offer me — for I might live to a hundred and
190   never see the principal.

CHARLES SURFACE. Oh, yes, you would! the moment Sir
Oliver dies, you know, you would come on me for the
money.

SIR OLIVER. Then I believe I should be the most un-
welcome dun you ever had in your life.

CHARLES SURFACE. What! I suppose you're afraid that Sir
Oliver is too good a life?

SIR OLIVER. No, indeed I am not; though I have heard he is
as hale and healthy as any man of his years in Christendom.

200 CHARLES SURFACE. There again, now, you are misinformed.
No, no, the climate has hurt him considerably, poor uncle
Oliver. Yes, yes, he breaks apace, I'm told — and is so
much altered lately that his nearest relations would not
know him.

SIR OLIVER. No! Ha! ha! ha! so much altered lately that his
nearest relations would not know him! Ha! ha! ha! egad —
ha! ha! ha!

CHARLES SURFACE. Ha! ha! — you're glad to hear that, little
Premium?

210 SIR OLIVER. No, no, I'm not.

CHARLES SURFACE. Yes, yes, you are — ha! ha! ha! — you
know that mends your chance.

SIR OLIVER. But I'm told Sir Oliver is coming over; nay,
some say he is actually arrived.

CHARLES SURFACE. Pshaw! sure I must know better than you whether he's come or not. No, no, rely on't he's at this moment at Calcutta. Isn't he, Moses?

MOSES. Oh, yes, certainly.

SIR OLIVER. Very true, as you say, you must know better than I, though I have it from pretty good authority. 220 Haven't I, Moses?

MOSES. Yes, most undoubted!

SIR OLIVER. But, sir, as I understand you want a few hundreds immediately, is there nothing you could dispose of?

CHARLES SURFACE. How do you mean?

SIR OLIVER. For instance, now, I have heard that your father left behind him a great quantity of massy old plate.

CHARLES SURFACE. O Lud! that's gone long ago. Moses can tell you how better than I can.

SIR OLIVER. [Aside]. Good lack! all the family race-cups 230 and corporation-bowls! — [Aloud.] Then it was also supposed that his library was one of the most valuable and compact.

CHARLES SURFACE. Yes, yes, so it was — vastly too much so for a private gentleman. For my part, I was always of a communicative disposition, so I thought it a shame to keep so much knowledge to myself.

SIR OLIVER. [Aside]. Mercy upon me! learning that had run in the family like an heir-loom! — [Aloud.] Pray, what are become of the books?   240

CHARLES SURFACE. You must inquire of the auctioneer, Master Premium, for I don't believe even Moses can direct you.

MOSES. I know nothing of books.

---

ll.230-1 the family race-cups and corporation-bowls: *race-cups won by the family and bowls presented to them by city corporations.*

SIR OLIVER. So, so, nothing of the family property left, I suppose?

CHARLES SURFACE. Not much, indeed; unless you have a mind to the family pictures. I have got a room full of ancestors above; and if you have a taste for old paintings, 250 egad, you shall have 'em a bargain!

SIR OLIVER. Hey! what the devil! sure, you wouldn't sell your forefathers, would you?

CHARLES SURFACE. Every man of them, to the best bidder.

SIR OLIVER. What! your great-uncles and aunts?

CHARLES SURFACE. Ay, and my great-grandfathers and grandmothers too.

SIR OLIVER. [*Aside*]. Now I give him up! — [*Aloud.*] What the plague, have you no bowels for your own kindred? Odds life! do you take me for Shylock in the play, that you 260 would raise money of me on your own flesh and blood?

CHARLES SURFACE. Nay, my little broker, don't be angry: what need you care, if you have your money's worth?

SIR OLIVER. Well, I'll be the purchaser: I think I can dispose of the family canvas. — [*Aside.*] Oh, I'll never forgive him this! never!

Re-enter CARELESS

CARELESS. Come, Charles, what keeps you?

CHARLES SURFACE. I can't come yet. I' faith, we are going to have a sale above stairs; here's little Premium will buy all my ancestors!

270 CARELESS. Oh, burn your ancestors!

CHARLES SURFACE. No, he may do that afterwards, if he pleases. Stay, Careless, we want you: egad, you shall be auctioneer — so come along with us.

CARELESS. Oh, have with you, if that's the case. I can handle a hammer as well as a dice-box! Going! going!

l.259 in the play: *in Shakespeare's* The Merchant of Venice.

SIR OLIVER. [*Aside*]. Oh, the profligates!

CHARLES SURFACE. Come, Moses, you shall be appraiser, if we want one. Gad's life, little Premium, you don't seem to like the business?

SIR OLIVER. Oh, yes, I do, vastly! Ha! ha! ha! yes, yes, I 280 think it a rare joke to sell one's family by auction — ha! ha! — [*Aside*.] Oh, the prodigal!

CHARLES SURFACE. To be sure! when a man wants money, where the plague should he get assistance, if he can't make free with his own relations!   [*Exeunt.*

SIR OLIVER. I'll never forgive him; never! never!

ACT IV

SCENE I. *The Picture Room in Charles Surface's House*

Enter CHARLES SURFACE, SIR OLIVER SURFACE, MOSES, *and* CARELESS

CHARLES SURFACE. Walk in, gentlemen, pray walk in; — here they are, the family of the Surfaces, up to the Conquest.

SIR OLIVER. And, in my opinion, a goodly collection.

CHARLES SURFACE. Ay, ay, these are done in the true spirit of portrait-painting; no *volontière grace* or expression. Not like the works of your modern Raphaels, who give you the strongest resemblance, yet contrive to make your portrait independent of you; so that you may sink the original and not hurt the picture. No, no; the merit of 10 these is the inveterate likeness — all stiff and awkward as the originals, and like nothing in human nature besides.

---

l.277 appraiser: *valuer*.
l.6 volontière grace: *affected grace*.
l.7 your modern Raphaels: *the famous Italian painter of the Renaissance*.

SIR OLIVER. Ah! we shall never see such figures of men again.

CHARLES SURFACE. I hope not. Well, you see, Master Premium, what a domestic character I am; here I sit of an evening surrounded by my family. But come, get to your pulpit, Mr. Auctioneer; here's an old gouty chair of my grandfather's will answer the purpose.

20 CARELESS. Ay, ay, this will do. But, Charles, I haven't a hammer; and what's an auctioneer without his hammer?

CHARLES SURFACE. Egad, that's true. What parchment have we here? Oh, our genealogy in full. [*Taking pedigree down.*] Here, Careless, you shall have no common bit of mahogany, here's the family tree for you, you rogue! This shall be your hammer, and now you may knock down my ancestors with their own pedigree.

SIR OLIVER. [*Aside*]. What an unnatural rogue! — an *ex post facto* parricide!

30 CARELESS. Yes, yes, here's a list of your generation indeed; — faith, Charles, this is the most convenient thing you could have found for the business, for 'twill not only serve as a hammer, but a catalogue into the bargain. Come, begin — A-going, a-going, a-going!

CHARLES SURFACE. Bravo, Careless! Well, here's my great-uncle, Sir Richard Raveline, a marvellous good general in his day, I assure you. He served in all the Duke of Marlborough's wars, and got that cut over his eye at the battle of Malplaquet. What say you, Mr. Premium? Look at
40   him — there's a hero! not cut out of his feathers, as your modern clipped captains are, but enveloped in wig and regimentals, as a general should be. What do you bid?

---

ll.28-9 ex post facto parricide: *a killer of his ancestors after they are dead.*
ll.37-8 the Duke of Marlborough's wars: *fought against the French in Queen Anne's reign. Malplaquet is one of Marlborough's famous victories.*

SIR OLIVER. [*Aside to* MOSES]. Bid him speak.

MOSES. Mr. Premium would have you speak.

CHARLES SURFACE. Why, then, he shall have him for ten pounds, and I'm sure that's not dear for a staff-officer.

SIR OLIVER. [*Aside*]. Heaven deliver me! his famous uncle Richard for ten pounds! [*Aloud.*] Very well, sir, I take him at that.

CHARLES SURFACE. Careless, knock down my uncle Richard. 50 — Here, now, is a maiden sister of his, my great-aunt Deborah, done by Kneller, in his best manner, and esteemed a very formidable likeness. There she is, you see, a shepherdess feeding her flock. You shall have her for five pounds ten — the sheep are worth the money.

SIR OLIVER. [*Aside*]. Ah! poor Deborah! a woman who set such a value on herself! [*Aloud.*] Five pounds ten — she's mine.

CHARLES SURFACE. Knock down my aunt Deborah! Here, now, are two that were a sort of cousins of theirs. — You 60 see, Moses, these pictures were done some time ago, when beaux wore wigs, and the ladies their own hair.

SIR OLIVER. Yes, truly, head-dresses appear to have been a little lower in those days.

CHARLES SURFACE. Well, take that couple for the same.

MOSES. 'Tis a good bargain.

CHARLES SURFACE. Careless! — This, now, is a grandfather of my mother's, a learned judge, well known on the western circuit. — What do you rate him at, Moses?

MOSES. Four guineas.   70

---

l.52. Kneller: *Sir Godfrey Kneller* (1648-1723), *a famous portrait painter*.
ll.61-2 when beaux wore wigs and ladies their own hair: *round about* 1700 *fashionable men wore full wigs and ladies dressed their own hair. By* 1777 (*the date of* The School for Scandal) *men had largely given up wigs, but ladies still made great use of false hair.*

CHARLES SURFACE. Four guineas! Gad's life, you don't bid me the price of his wig. — Mr. Premium, you have more respect for the Woolsack; do let us knock his lordship down at fifteen.

SIR OLIVER. By all means.

CARELESS. Gone!

CHARLES SURFACE. And there are two brothers of his, William and Walter Blunt, Esquires, both members of Parliament, and noted speakers; and, what's very extra-
80 ordinary, I believe, this is the first time they were ever bought or sold.

SIR OLIVER. That is very extraordinary, indeed! I'll take them at your own price, for the honour of Parliament.

CARELESS. Well said, little Premium! I'll knock them down at forty.

CHARLES SURFACE. Here's a jolly fellow — I don't know what relation, but he was mayor of Norwich: take him at eight pounds.

SIR OLIVER. No, no; six will do for the mayor.

90 CHARLES SURFACE. Come, make it guineas, and I'll throw you the two aldermen there into the bargain.

SIR OLIVER. They're mine.

CHARLES SURFACE. Careless, knock down the mayor and aldermen. But, plague on't! we shall be all day retailing in this manner; do let us deal wholesale: what say you, little Premium? Give me three hundred pounds for the rest of the family in the lump.

CARELESS. Ay, ay, that will be the best way.

SIR OLIVER. Well, well, anything to accommodate you; they
100 are mine. But there is one portrait which you have always passed over.

---

l.73 the Woolsack: *the seat of the Lord Chancellor in the House of Lords.*

CARELESS. What, that ill-looking little fellow over the settee.

SIR OLIVER. Yes, sir, I mean that; though I don't think him so ill-looking a little fellow, by any means.

CHARLES SURFACE. What, that? Oh; that's my uncle Oliver! 'twas done before he went to India.

CARELESS. Your uncle Oliver! Gad, then you'll never be friends, Charles. That, now, to me, is as stern a looking rogue as ever I saw; an unforgiving eye, and a damned dis-inheriting countenance! an inveterate knave, depend on't. 110 Don't you think so, little Premium?

SIR OLIVER. Upon my soul, sir, I do not; I think it is as honest a looking face as any in the room, dead or alive. But I suppose uncle Oliver goes with the rest of the lumber?

CHARLES SURFACE. No, hang it! I'll not part with poor Noll. The old fellow has been very good to me, and, egad, I'll keep his picture while I've a room to put it in.

SIR OLIVER. [Aside]. The rogue's my nephew after all! — [Aloud.] But, sir, I have somehow taken a fancy to that 120 picture.

CHARLES SURFACE. I'm sorry for't, for you certainly will not have it. Oons, haven't you got enough of them?

SIR OLIVER. [Aside]. I forgive him every thing! [Aloud.] But, sir, when I take a whim in my head, I don't value money. I'll give you as much for that as for all the rest.

CHARLES SURFACE. Don't tease me, master broker; I tell you I'll not part with it, and there's an end of it.

SIR OLIVER. [Aside]. How like his father the dog is! — [Aloud.] Well, well, I have done. — [Aside.] I did not 130 perceive it before, but I think I never saw such a striking resemblance. — [Aloud.] Here is a draft for your sum.

CHARLES SURFACE. Why, 'tis for eight hundred pounds!

SIR OLIVER. You will not let Sir Oliver go?

CHARLES SURFACE. Zounds! no! I tell you, once more.

SIR OLIVER. Then never mind the difference, we'll balance that another time. But give me your hand on the bargain; you are an honest fellow, Charles — I beg pardon, sir, for being so free. — Come, Moses.

140 CHARLES SURFACE. Egad, this is a whimsical old fellow! — But hark'ee, Premium, you'll prepare lodgings for these gentlemen.

SIR OLIVER. Yes, yes, I'll send for them in a day or two.

CHARLES SURFACE. But hold; do now send a genteel conveyance for them, for, I assure you, they were most of them used to ride in their own carriages.

SIR OLIVER. I will, I will — for all but Oliver.

CHARLES SURFACE. Ay, all but the little nabob.

SIR OLIVER. You're fixed on that?

150 CHARLES SURFACE. Peremptorily.

SIR OLIVER. [Aside]. A dear extravagant rogue! — [Aloud.] Good day! — Come, Moses. — [Aside.] Let me hear now who dares call him profligate.   [Exit with MOSES.

CARELESS. Why, this is the oddest genius of the sort I ever met with!

CHARLES SURFACE. Egad, he's the prince of brokers, I think. I wonder how the devil Moses got acquainted with so honest a fellow. — Ha! here's Rowley. — Do, Careless, say I'll join the company in a few moments.

160 CARELESS. I will — but don't let that old blockhead persuade you to squander any of that money on old musty debts, or any such nonsense; for tradesmen, Charles, are the most exorbitant fellows.

CHARLES SURFACE. Very true, and paying them is only encouraging them.

---

l.148 the little nabob: *a term used of any very wealthy person who returned to Europe from the East.*
l.150 Peremptorily: *absolutely.*
l.154 genius: *character.*

CARELESS. Nothing else.

CHARLES SURFACE. Ay, ay, never fear. — [*Exit* CARELESS.] So! this was an odd old fellow, indeed. Let me see, two-thirds of these five hundred and thirty odd pounds are mine by right. 'Fore heavens! I find one's ancestors are 170 more valuable relations than I took them for! — Ladies and gentlemen, your most obedient and very grateful servant.
[*Bows ceremoniously to the pictures.*

Enter ROWLEY

Ha! old Rowley! egad, you are just come in time to take leave of your old acquaintance.

ROWLEY. Yes, I heard they were a-going. But I wonder you can have such spirits under so many distresses.

CHARLES SURFACE. Why, there's the point! my distresses are so many, that I can't afford to part with my spirits; but I shall be rich and splenetic, all in good time. How-ever, I suppose you are surprised that I am not more sor- 180 rowful at parting with so many near relations; to be sure, 'tis very affecting, but you see they never move a muscle, so why should I?

ROWLEY. There's no making you serious a moment.

CHARLES SURFACE. Yes, faith, I am so now. Here, my honest Rowley, here, get me this changed directly, and take a hundred pounds of it immediately to old Stanley.

ROWLEY. A hundred pounds! Consider only ——

CHARLES SURFACE. Gad's life, don't talk about it! poor Stanley's wants are pressing, and, if you don't make haste, 190 we shall have some one call that has a better right to the money.

ROWLEY. Ah! there's the point! I never will cease dunning you with the old proverb ——

---

l.179 splenetic: *full of spleen; testy.*

CHARLES SURFACE. *Be just before you're generous.* — Why, so I would if I could; but Justice is an old, hobbling beldame, and I can't get her to keep pace with Generosity, for the soul of me.

ROWLEY. Yet, Charles, believe me, one hour's reflection ——

200 CHARLES SURFACE. Ay, ay, it's very true; but, hark'ee, Rowley, while I have, by Heaven I'll give; and now for hazard.   [*Exeunt.*

SCENE II. *Another Room in the same*

Enter SIR OLIVER SURFACE *and* MOSES

MOSES. Well, sir, I think, as Sir Peter said, you have seen Mr. Charles in high glory; 'tis great pity he's so extravagant.

SIR OLIVER. True, but he would not sell my picture.

MOSES. And loves wine and women so much.

SIR OLIVER. But he would not sell my picture.

MOSES. And games so deep.

SIR OLIVER. But he would not sell my picture. Oh, here's Rowley.

Enter ROWLEY

10 ROWLEY. So, Sir Oliver, I find you have made a purchase ——

SIR OLIVER. Yes, yes, our young rake has parted with his ancestors like old tapestry.

ROWLEY. And here has he commissioned me to re-deliver you part of the purchase money — I mean, though, in your necessitous character of old Stanley.

MOSES. Ah! there is the pity of all; he is so damned charitable.

---

l.196 beldame: *hag.*

ROWLEY. And I left a hosier and two tailors in the hall, who, I'm sure, won't be paid, and this hundred would satisfy them.   20

SIR OLIVER. Well, well, I'll pay his debts, and his benevolence too. But now I am no more a broker, and you shall introduce me to the elder brother as old Stanley.

ROWLEY. Not yet awhile; Sir Peter, I know, means to call there about this time.

Enter TRIP

TRIP. Oh, gentlemen, I beg pardon for not showing you out; this way — Moses, a word.   [*Exit with* MOSES.

SIR OLIVER. There's a fellow for you! Would you believe it, that puppy intercepted the Jew on our coming, and wanted to raise money before he got to his master!   30

ROWLEY. Indeed!

SIR OLIVER. Yes, they are now planning an annuity business, Ah, Master Rowley, in my days servants were content with the follies of their masters, when they were worn a little threadbare; but now they have their vices like their birthday clothes, with the gloss on.   [*Exeunt.*

SCENE III. *A Library in Joseph Surface's House*

Enter JOSEPH SURFACE *and* SERVANT

JOSEPH SURFACE. No letter from Lady Teazle?

SERVANT. No, sir.

JOSEPH SURFACE. [*Aside*]. I am surprised she has not sent, if she is prevented from coming. Sir Peter certainly does not suspect me. Yet I wish I may not lose the heiress, through the scrape I have drawn myself into with the wife; however, Charles's imprudence and bad character are great points in my favour.   [*Knocking without.*

1.18 a hosier: *a hosier deals in hose, stockings, and ready-made garments.*

SERVANT. Sir, I believe that must be Lady Teazle.

10 JOSEPH SURFACE. Hold! See whether it is or not, before you go to the door: I have a particular message for you, if it should be my brother.

SERVANT. 'Tis her ladyship, sir; she always leaves her chair at the milliner's in the next street.

JOSEPH SURFACE. Stay, stay; draw that screen before the window — that will do; — my opposite neighbour is a maiden lady of so curious a temper. [SERVANT *draws the screen, and exit.*] I have a difficult hand to play in this affair. Lady Teazle has lately suspected my views on 20 Maria; but she must by no means be let into that secret, — at least, till I have her more in my power.

Enter LADY TEAZLE

LADY TEAZLE. What, sentiment in soliloquy now? Have you been very impatient? O Lud! don't pretend to look grave. I vow I couldn't come before.

JOSEPH SURFACE. O madam, punctuality is a species of constancy very unfashionable in a lady of quality.
    [*Places chairs, and sits after* LADY TEAZLE *is seated.*

LADY TEAZLE. Upon my word, you ought to pity me. Do you know Sir Peter is grown so ill-natured to me of late, and so jealous of Charles too — that's the best of the 30 story, isn't it?

JOSEPH SURFACE. [*Aside*]. I am glad my scandalous friends keep that up.

LADY TEAZLE. I am sure I wish he would let Maria marry him, and then perhaps he would be convinced; don't you, Mr. Surface?

---

l.14 the milliner's: *dress shop; haberdasher.*
l.22 sentiment in soliloquy: '*You are giving vent to all your fine thoughts on your own.*'
l.25 species of constancy: *kind of devotedness.*

JOSEPH SURFACE. [*Aside*]. Indeed I do not. — [*Aloud*.] Oh,
certainly I do! for then my dear Lady Teazle would also
be convinced how wrong her suspicions were of my having
any design on the silly girl.

LADY TEAZLE. Well, well, I'm inclined to believe you. But 40
isn't it provoking, to have the most ill-natured things said
of one? And there's my friend Lady Sneerwell has circulated I don't know how many scandalous tales of me,
and all without any foundation too; that's what vexes me.

JOSEPH SURFACE. Ay, madam, to be sure, that is the provoking circumstance — without foundation; yes, yes,
there's the mortification, indeed; for when a scandalous
story is believed against one, there certainly is no comfort
like the consciousness of having deserved it.

LADY TEAZLE. No, to be sure, then I'd forgive their malice; 50
but to attack me, who am really so innocent, and who
never say an ill-natured thing of anybody — that is, of any
friend; and then Sir Peter, too, to have him so peevish,
and so suspicious, when I know the integrity of my own
heart — indeed 'tis monstrous!

JOSEPH SURFACE. But, my dear Lady Teazle, 'tis your own
fault if you suffer it. When a husband entertains a ground-
less suspicion of his wife, and withdraws his confidence
from her, the original compact is broken, and she owes it
to the honour of her sex to endeavour to outwit him.   60

LADY TEAZLE. Indeed! So that, if he suspects me without
cause, it follows, that the best way of curing his jealousy is
to give him reason for't?

JOSEPH SURFACE. Undoubtedly — for your husband should
never be deceived in you: and in that case it becomes you
to be frail in compliment to his discernment.

LADY TEAZLE. To be sure, what you say is very reasonable,
and when the consciousness of my innocence ——

JOSEPH SURFACE. Ah, my dear madam, there is the great
mistake! 'tis this very conscious innocence that is of the 70

greatest prejudice to you. What is it makes you negligent of forms, and careless of the world's opinion? why, the consciousness of your own innocence. What makes you thoughtless in your conduct, and apt to run into a thousand little imprudences? why, the consciousness of your own innocence. What makes you impatient of Sir Peter's temper, and outrageous at his suspicions? why, the consciousness of your own innocence.

LADY TEAZLE. 'Tis very true!

80 JOSEPH SURFACE. Now, my dear Lady Teazle, if you would but once make a trifling *faux pas*, you can't conceive how cautious you would grow, and how ready to humour and agree with your husband.

LADY TEAZLE. Do you think so?

JOSEPH SURFACE. Oh, I am sure on't; and then you would find all scandal would cease at once, for — in short, your character at present is like a person in a plethora, absolutely dying from too much health.

LADY TEAZLE. So, so; then I perceive your prescription is,
90 that I must sin in my own defence, and part with my virtue to preserve my reputation?

JOSEPH SURFACE. Exactly so, upon my credit, ma'am.

LADY TEAZLE. Well, certainly this is the oddest doctrine, and the newest receipt for avoiding calumny!

JOSEPH SURFACE. An infallible one, believe me. Prudence, like experience, must be paid for.

LADY TEAZLE. Why, if my understanding were once convinced ——

JOSEPH SURFACE. Oh, certainly, madam, your understand-
100 ing should be convinced. Yes, yes — Heaven forbid I

---

l.81 faux pas: *mistake.*
l.87 a plethora: *ill-health caused by too much blood: the opposite to anaemia.*
l.94 calumny: *false tales about a person.*

should persuade you to do anything you thought wrong. No, no, I have too much honour to desire it.

LADY TEAZLE. Don't you think we may as well leave honour out of the argument? [*Rises.*

JOSEPH SURFACE. Ah, the ill effects of your country education, I see, still remain with you.

LADY TEAZLE. I doubt they do indeed; and I will fairly own to you, that if I could be persuaded to do wrong, it would be by Sir Peter's ill usage sooner than your honourable logic, after all. 110

JOSEPH SURFACE. Then, by this hand, which he is unworthy of —— [*Taking her hand.*

Re-enter SERVANT

'Sdeath, you blockhead — what do you want?

SERVANT. I beg your pardon, sir, but I thought you would not choose Sir Peter to come up without announcing him.

JOSEPH SURFACE. Sir Peter! — Oons — the devil!

LADY TEAZLE. Sir Peter! O Lud! I'm ruined! I'm ruined!

SERVANT. Sir, 'twasn't I let him in.

LADY TEAZLE. Oh! I'm quite undone! What will become of me? Now, Mr. Logic — Oh! mercy, sir, he's on the 120 stairs — I'll get behind here — and if ever I'm so imprudent again —— [*Goes behind the screen.*

JOSEPH SURFACE. Give me that book.
[*Sits down.* SERVANT *pretends to adjust his chair.*

Enter SIR PETER TEAZLE

SIR PETER. Ay, ever improving himself — Mr. Surface, Mr. Surface —— [*Pats* JOSEPH *on the shoulder.*

JOSEPH SURFACE. Oh, my dear Sir Peter, I beg your pardon. — [*Gaping, throws away the book.*] I have been dozing over a stupid book. Well, I am much obliged to you for this call. You haven't been here, I believe, since I fitted

130 up this room. Books, you know, are the only things I am
a coxcomb in.

SIR PETER. 'Tis very neat indeed. Well, well, that's proper;
and you can make even your screen a source of knowledge — hung, I perceive, with maps.

JOSEPH SURFACE. Oh, yes, I find great use in that screen.

SIR PETER. I dare say you must, certainly, when you want to
find anything in a hurry.

JOSEPH SURFACE. [*Aside*]. Ay, or to hide anything in a
hurry either.

140 SIR PETER. Well, I have a little private business ——

JOSEPH SURFACE. You need not stay.   [*To* SERVANT.

SERVANT. No, sir.   [*Exit.*

JOSEPH SURFACE. Here's a chair, Sir Peter — I beg ——

SIR PETER. Well, now we are alone, there is a subject, my
dear friend, on which I wish to unburden my mind to you
— a point of the greatest moment to my peace; in short,
my good friend, Lady Teazle's conduct of late has made
me very unhappy.

JOSEPH SURFACE. Indeed! I am very sorry to hear it.

150 SIR PETER. 'Tis but too plain she has not the least regard for
me; but, what's worse, I have pretty good authority to
suppose she has formed an attachment to another.

JOSEPH SURFACE. Indeed! you astonish me!

SIR PETER. Yes! and, between ourselves, I think I've discovered the person.

JOSEPH SURFACE. How! you alarm me exceedingly.

SIR PETER. Ay, my dear friend, I knew you would sym-
pathise with me!

JOSEPH SURFACE. Yes, believe me, Sir Peter, such a dis-
160 covery would hurt me just as much as it would you.

---

l.131 coxcomb: *a showy fellow.*

SIR PETER. I am convinced of it. Ah! it is a happiness to have a friend whom we can trust even with one's family secrets. But have you no guess who I mean?

JOSEPH SURFACE. I haven't the most distant idea. It can't be Sir Benjamin Backbite!

SIR PETER. Oh, no! What say you to Charles?

JOSEPH SURFACE. My brother! impossible!

SIR PETER. Oh, my dear friend, the goodness of your own heart misleads you. You judge of others by yourself.

JOSEPH SURFACE. Certainly, Sir Peter, the heart that is 170 conscious of its own integrity is ever slow to credit another's treachery.

SIR PETER. True; but your brother has no sentiment — you never hear him talk so.

JOSEPH SURFACE. Yet I can't but think Lady Teazle herself has too much principle.

SIR PETER. Ay; but what is principle against the flattery of a handsome, lively young fellow?

JOSEPH SURFACE. That's very true.

SIR PETER. And then, you know, the difference of our ages 180 makes it very improbable that she should have any great affection for me; and if she were to be frail, and I were to make it public, why the town would only laugh at me, the foolish old bachelor, who had married a girl.

JOSEPH SURFACE. That's true, to be sure — they would laugh.

SIR PETER. Laugh! ay, and make ballads, and paragraphs, and the devil knows what of me.

JOSEPH SURFACE. No, you must never make it public.

---

l.173 sentiment: *sensitivity to another person's feelings.*
l.182 frail: *deceive her husband.*
l.187 paragraphs: *in the newspapers.*

190 SIR PETER. But then again — that the nephew of my old friend, Sir Oliver, should be the person to attempt such a wrong, hurts me more nearly.

JOSEPH SURFACE. Ay, there's the point. When ingratitude barbs the dart of injury, the wound has double danger in it.

SIR PETER. Ay — I, that was, in a manner, left his guardian; in whose house he had been so often entertained; who never in my life denied him — my advice!

JOSEPH SURFACE. Oh, 'tis not to be credited! There may be a man capable of such baseness, to be sure; but, for my 200 part, till you can give me positive proofs, I cannot but doubt it. However, if it should be proved on him, he is no longer a brother of mine — I disclaim kindred with him: for the man who can break the laws of hospitality, and tempt the wife of his friend, deserves to be branded as the pest of society.

SIR PETER. What a difference there is between you! What noble sentiments!

JOSEPH SURFACE. Yet I cannot suspect Lady Teazle's honour.

210 SIR PETER. I am sure I wish to think well of her, and to remove all grounds of quarrel between us. She has lately reproached me more than once with having made no settlement on her; and, in our last quarrel, she almost hinted that she should not break her heart if I was dead. Now, as we seem to differ in our ideas of expense, I have resolved she shall have her own way, and be her own mistress in that respect for the future; and, if I were to die, she will find I have not been inattentive to her interest while living. Here, my friend, are the drafts of two 220 deeds, which I wish to have your opinion on. By one, she will enjoy eight hundred a year independent while I live, and, by the other, the bulk of my fortune at my death.

---

l.213 settlement: *made money over to her legally*.
l.220 deeds: *legal documents*.

JOSEPH SURFACE. This conduct, Sir Peter, is indeed truly generous. — [*Aside.*] I wish it may not corrupt my pupil.

SIR PETER. Yes, I am determined she shall have no cause to complain, though I would not have her acquainted with the latter instance of my affection yet awhile.

JOSEPH SURFACE. [*Aside*]. Nor I, if I could help it.

SIR PETER. And now, my dear friend, if you please, we will talk over the situation of your hopes with Maria.   230

JOSEPH SURFACE. [*Softly*]. Oh, no, Sir Peter; another time, if you please.

SIR PETER. I am sensibly chagrined at the little progress you seem to make in her affections.

JOSEPH SURFACE. [*Softly*]. I beg you will not mention it. What are my disappointments when your happiness is in debate! — [*Aside.*] 'Sdeath, I shall be ruined every way!

SIR PETER. And though you are averse to my acquainting Lady Teazle with your passion, I'm sure she's not your enemy in the affair.   240

JOSEPH SURFACE. Pray, Sir Peter, now oblige me. I am really too much affected by the subject we have been speaking of to bestow a thought on my own concerns. The man who is entrusted with his friend's distresses can never ——

Re-enter SERVANT

Well sir?

SERVANT. Your brother, sir, is speaking to a gentleman in the street, and says he knows you are within.

JOSEPH SURFACE. 'Sdeath, blockhead, I'm not within — I'm out for the day.

SIR PETER. Stay — hold — a thought has struck me — you 250 shall be at home.

JOSEPH SURFACE. Well, well, let him come up. — [*Exit* SERVANT.] [*Aside*]. He'll interrupt Sir Peter, however.

SIR PETER. Now, my good friend, oblige me, I entreat you. Before Charles comes, let me conceal myself somewhere, then do you tax him on the point we have been talking, and his answer may satisfy me at once.

JOSEPH SURFACE. Oh, fie, Sir Peter! would you have me join in so mean a trick? — to trepan my brother too?

260 SIR PETER. Nay, you tell me you are sure he is innocent; if so, you do him the greatest service by giving him an opportunity to clear himself, and you will set my heart at rest. Come, you shall not refuse me: [*Going up,*] here, behind the screen will be — Hey! what the devil! there seems to be one listener here already — I'll swear I saw a petticoat!

JOSEPH SURFACE. Ha! ha! ha! Well, this is ridiculous enough. I'll tell you, Sir Peter, though I hold a man of intrigue to be a most despicable character, yet, you know,
270 it does not follow that one is to be an absolute Joseph either! Hark'ee, 'tis a little French milliner, a silly rogue that plagues me; and having some character to lose, on your coming, sir, she ran behind the screen.

SIR PETER. Ah, Joseph! Joseph! Did I ever think that you —— But, egad, she has overheard all I have been saying of my wife.

JOSEPH SURFACE. Oh, 'twill never go any farther, you may depend upon it!

SIR PETER. No! then, faith, let her hear it out. — Here's a
280 closet will do as well.

JOSEPH SURFACE. Well, go in there.

SIR PETER. Sly rogue! sly rogue!   [*Goes into the closet.*

JOSEPH SURFACE. A narrow escape, indeed! and a curious situation I'm in, to part man and wife in this manner.

LADY TEAZLE. [*Peeping*]. Couldn't I steal off?

JOSEPH SURFACE. Keep close, my angel!

---

l.259 to trepan: *trap, trick.*
l.270 an absolute Joseph: *a model of righteous conduct like Joseph in the Old Testament.*

SIR PETER. [*Peeping*]. Joseph, tax him home.

JOSEPH SURFACE. Back, my dear friend!

LADY TEAZLE. [*Peeping*]. Couldn't you lock Sir Peter in?

JOSEPH SURFACE. Be still, my life!   290

SIR PETER. [*Peeping*]. You're sure the little milliner won't blab?

JOSEPH SURFACE. In, in, my dear Sir Peter! — 'Fore Gad, I wish I had a key to the door.

Enter CHARLES SURFACE

CHARLES SURFACE. Holla! brother, what has been the matter? Your fellow would not let me up at first. What! have you had a Jew with you?

JOSEPH SURFACE. No, brother, I assure you.

CHARLES SURFACE. But what has made Sir Peter steal off? I thought he had been with you.   300

JOSEPH SURFACE. He was, brother; but, hearing you were coming, he did not choose to stay.

CHARLES SURFACE. What! was the old gentleman afraid I wanted to borrow money of him?

JOSEPH SURFACE. No, sir: but I am sorry to find, Charles, you have lately given that worthy man grounds for great uneasiness.

CHARLES SURFACE. Yes, they tell me I do that to a great many worthy men. But how so, pray?

JOSEPH SURFACE. To be plain with you, brother, he thinks 310 you are endeavouring to gain Lady Teazle's affections from him.

CHARLES SURFACE. Who, I? O Lud! not I, upon my word. — Ha! ha! ha! ha! so the old fellow has found out that he has got a young wife, has he? — or, what is worse, Lady Teazle has found out she has an old husband?

JOSEPH SURFACE. This is no subject to jest on, brother. He who can laugh ——

CHARLES SURFACE. True, true, as you were going to say —
320 then, seriously, I never had the least idea of what you charge me with, upon my honour.

JOSEPH SURFACE. [*Raising his voice*]. Well, it will give Sir Peter great satisfaction to hear this.

CHARLES SURFACE. To be sure, I once thought the lady seemed to have taken a fancy to me; but, upon my soul, I never gave her the least encouragement. Besides, you know my attachment to Maria.

JOSEPH SURFACE. But sure, brother, even if Lady Teazle had betrayed the fondest partiality for you ——

330 CHARLES SURFACE. Why, look'ee, Joseph, I hope I shall never deliberately do a dishonourable action; but if a pretty woman was purposely to throw herself in my way — and that pretty woman married to a man old enough to be her father ——

JOSEPH SURFACE. Well!

CHARLES SURFACE. Why, I believe I should be obliged to ——

JOSEPH SURFACE. What?

CHARLES SURFACE. To borrow a little of your morality, that's all. But, brother, do you know now that you surprise
340 me exceedingly, by naming me with Lady Teazle; for, i' faith, I always understood you were her favourite.

JOSEPH SURFACE. Oh, for shame, Charles! This retort is foolish.

CHARLES SURFACE. Nay, I swear I have seen you exchange such significant glances ——

JOSEPH SURFACE. Nay, nay, sir, this is no jest.

CHARLES SURFACE. Egad, I'm serious! Don't you remember one day, when I called here ——

JOSEPH SURFACE. Nay, pr'ythee, Charles ——

350 CHARLES SURFACE. And found you together ——

JOSEPH SURFACE. Zounds, sir, I insist ——

CHARLES SURFACE. And another time when your servant ——

JOSEPH SURFACE. Brother, brother, a word with you! — [*Aside.*] Gad, I must stop him.

CHARLES SURFACE. Informed, I say, that ——

JOSEPH SURFACE. Hush! I beg your pardon, but Sir Peter has overheard all we have been saying. I knew you would clear yourself, or I should not have consented.

CHARLES SURFACE. How, Sir Peter! Where is he?

JOSEPH SURFACE. Softly, there!   [*Points to the closet.* 360

CHARLES SURFACE. Oh, 'fore Heaven, I'll have him out. Sir Peter, come forth!

JOSEPH SURFACE. No, no ——

CHARLES SURFACE. I say, Sir Peter, come into court. — [*Pulls in* SIR PETER.] What! my old guardian! — What! turn inquisitor, and take evidence incog.? Oh, fie! Oh, fie!

SIR PETER. Give me your hand, Charles — I believe I have suspected you wrongfully; but you mustn't be angry with Joseph — 'twas my plan!   370

CHARLES SURFACE. Indeed!

SIR PETER. But I acquit you. I promise you I don't think near so ill of you as I did: what I have heard has given me great satisfaction.

CHARLES SURFACE. Egad, then, 'twas lucky you didn't hear any more. Wasn't it, Joseph?

SIR PETER. Ah! you would have retorted on him.

CHARLES SURFACE. Ah, ay, that was a joke.

SIR PETER. Yes, yes, I know his honour too well.

CHARLES SURFACE. But you might as well have suspected 380 him as me in this matter, for all that. Mightn't he, Joseph?

---

l.366 incog.: *incognito, in disguise.*
l.377 retorted: *answered in kind; given him tit for tat.*

SIR PETER. Well, well, I believe you.

JOSEPH SURFACE. [*Aside*]. Would they were both out of the room!

SIR PETER. And in future, perhaps, we may not be such strangers.

Re-enter SERVANT, *and whispers to* JOSEPH SURFACE

SERVANT. Lady Sneerwell is below, and says she will come up.

390 JOSEPH SURFACE. Lady Sneerwell! Gad's life! she must not come here. [*Exit* SERVANT.] Gentlemen, I beg pardon — I must wait on you down stairs: here is a person come on particular business.

CHARLES SURFACE. Well, you can see him in another room. Sir Peter and I have not met a long time, and I have something to say to him.

JOSEPH SURFACE. [*Aside*]. They must not be left together. — [*Aloud.*] I'll send Lady Sneerwell away, and return directly. — [*Aside to* SIR PETER.] Sir Peter, not a word of
400 the French milliner.

SIR PETER. [*Aside to* JOSEPH SURFACE]. I! Not for the world! [*Exit* JOSEPH SURFACE.] Ah, Charles, if you associated more with your brother, one might indeed hope for your reformation. He is a man of sentiment. Well, there is nothing in the world so noble as a man of sentiment.

CHARLES SURFACE. Pshaw! he is too moral by half; and so apprehensive of his good name, as he calls it.

SIR PETER. No, no, — come, come, — you wrong him. No,
410 no! Joseph is no rake, but he is so such saint either, in that respect. — [*Aside.*] I have a great mind to tell him — we should have such a laugh at Joseph.

---

l.404 a man of sentiment: *a man of the noblest feelings.*

CHARLES SURFACE. Oh, hang him! he's a very anchorite, a young hermit!

SIR PETER. Hark'ee — you must not abuse him: he may chance to hear of it again, I promise you.

CHARLES SURFACE. Why, you won't tell him?

SIR PETER. No — but — this way. — [*Aside.*] Egad, I'll tell him. — [*Aloud.*] Hark'ee — have you a mind to have a good laugh at Joseph?   420

CHARLES SURFACE. I should like it of all things.

SIR PETER. Then, i' faith, we will! I'll be quit with him for discovering me. [*Whispers*]. He had a girl with him when I called.

CHARLES SURFACE. What! Joseph? you jest.

SIR PETER. Hush! — a little French milliner — and the best of the jest is — she's in the room now.

CHARLES SURFACE. The devil she is!

SIR PETER. Hush! I tell you.   [*Points to the screen.*

CHARLES SURFACE. Behind the screen! 'Slife, let's unveil 430 her!

SIR PETER. No, no, he's coming: — you sha'n't, indeed!

CHARLES SURFACE. Oh, egad, we'll have a peep at the little milliner!

SIR PETER. Not for the world! — Joseph will never forgive me.

CHARLES SURFACE. I'll stand by you ——

SIR PETER. Odds, here he is!

>   [CHARLES SURFACE *throws down the screen.*
>   *Re-enter* JOSEPH SURFACE

CHARLES SURFACE. Lady Teazle, by all that's wonderful.

SIR PETER. Lady Teazle, by all that's damnable!   [440

1.413 anchorite: *one who renounces the world and retires into religious seclusion.*

CHARLES SURFACE. Sir Peter, this is one of the smartest French milliners I ever saw. Egad, you seem all to have been diverting yourselves here at hide and seek, and I don't see who is out of the secret. Shall I beg your ladyship to inform me? Not a word! — Brother, will you be pleased to explain this matter? What! is Morality dumb too? — Sir Peter, though I found you in the dark, perhaps you are not so now! All mute! — Well — though I can make nothing of the affair, I suppose you perfectly understand
450   one another; so I'll leave you to yourselves. [*Going.*] Brother, I'm sorry to find you have given that worthy man grounds for so much uneasiness. — Sir Peter! there's nothing in the world so noble as a man of senti-ment!   [*Exit.*

JOSEPH SURFACE. Sir Peter — notwithstanding — I confess — that appearances are against me — if you will afford me your patience — I make no doubt — but I shall explain every thing to your satisfaction.

SIR PETER. If you please, sir.

460 JOSEPH SURFACE. The fact is, sir, that Lady Teazle, know-ing my pretensions to your ward Maria — I say, sir, Lady Teazle, being apprehensive of the jealousy of your temper — and knowing my friendship to the family — she, sir, I say — called here — in order that — I might explain these pretensions — but on your coming — being appre-hensive — as I said — of your jealousy — she withdrew — and this, you may depend on it, is the whole truth of the matter.

SIR PETER. A very clear account, upon my word; and I dare
470   swear the lady will vouch for every article of it.

LADY TEAZLE. For not one word of it, Sir Peter!

SIR PETER. How! don't you think it worth while to agree in the lie?

LADY TEAZLE. There is not one syllable of truth in what that gentleman has told you.

SIR PETER. I believe you, upon my soul, ma'am!

JOSEPH SURFACE. [*Aside to* LADY TEAZLE]. S'death, madam, will you betray me?

LADY TEAZLE. Good Mr. Hypocrite, by your leave, I'll speak for myself.   480

SIR PETER. Ay, let her alone, sir; you'll find she'll make out a better story than you, without prompting.

LADY TEAZLE. Hear me, Sir Peter! — I came here on no matter relating to your ward, and even ignorant of this gentleman's pretensions to her. But I came, induced by his insidious arguments, at least to listen to his pretended passion.

SIR PETER. Now, I believe, the truth is coming, indeed!

JOSEPH SURFACE. The woman's mad!

LADY TEAZLE. No, sir; she has recovered her senses, and 490 your own arts have furnished her with the means. — Sir Peter, I do not expect you to credit me — but the tenderness you expressed for me, when I am sure you could not think I was a witness to it, has so penetrated to my heart, that I left the place without the shame of this discovery, my future life should have spoken the sincerity of my gratitude. As for that smooth-tongued hypocrite, I behold him now in a light so truly despicable, that I shall never again respect myself for having listened to him.   [*Exit.*

JOSEPH SURFACE. Notwithstanding all this, Sir Peter, 500 Heaven knows ——

SIR PETER. That you are a villain! and so I leave you to your conscience.

JOSEPH SURFACE. You are too rash, Sir Peter; you shall hear me. The man who shuts out conviction by refusing to ——

SIR PETER. Oh, damn your sentiments!
        [*Exeunt* SIR PETER *and* JOSEPH SURFACE, *talking.*

ACT V

SCENE I. *The Library in Joseph Surface's House*

Enter JOSEPH SURFACE *and* SERVANT

JOSEPH SURFACE. Mr. Stanley! and why should you think I would see him? you must know he comes to ask something.

SERVANT. Sir, I should not have let him in, but that Mr. Rowley came to the door with him.

JOSEPH SURFACE. Pshaw! blockhead! to suppose that I should now be in a temper to receive visits from poor relations! — Well, why don't you show the fellow up?

SERVANT. I will, sir. — Why, sir, it was not my fault that Sir
10 Peter discovered my lady ——

JOSEPH SURFACE. Go, fool! — [*Exit* SERVANT.] Sure Fortune never played a man of my policy such a trick before! My character with Sir Peter, my hopes with Maria, destroyed in a moment! I'm in a rare humour to listen to other people's distresses! I sha'n't be able to bestow even a benevolent sentiment on Stanley. — So! here he comes, and Rowley with him. I must try to recover myself, and put a little charity into my face, however.   [*Exit.*

Enter SIR OLIVER SURFACE *and* ROWLEY

SIR OLIVER. What! does he avoid us? That was he, was it
20 not?

ROWLEY. It was, sir. But I doubt you are come a little too abruptly. His nerves are so weak, that the sight of a poor relation may be too much for him. I should have gone first to break it to him.

SIR OLIVER. Oh, plague of his nerves! Yet this is he whom Sir Peter extols as a man of the most benevolent way of thinking!

---

l.16 benevolent sentiment: *some well-intentioned precepts or advice.*

ROWLEY. As to his way of thinking, I cannot pretend to decide; for, to do him justice, he appears to have as much speculative benevolence as any private gentleman in the 30 kingdom, though he is seldom so sensual as to indulge himself in the exercise of it.

SIR OLIVER. Yet he has a string of charitable sentiments at his fingers' ends.

ROWLEY. Or, rather, at his tongue's end, Sir Oliver; for I believe there is no sentiment he has such faith in as that *Charity begins at home.*

SIR OLIVER. And his, I presume, is of that domestic sort which never stirs abroad at all.

ROWLEY. I doubt you'll find it so; but he's coming. I 40 mustn't seem to interrupt you; and you know, immediately as you leave him, I come in to announce your arrival in your real character.

SIR OLIVER. True; and afterwards you'll meet me at Sir Peter's.

ROWLEY. Without losing a moment.   [*Exit.*

SIR OLIVER. I don't like the complaisance of his features.

Re-enter JOSEPH SURFACE

JOSEPH SURFACE. Sir, I beg you ten thousand pardons for keeping you a moment waiting. — Mr. Stanley, I presume. 50

SIR OLIVER. At your service.

JOSEPH SURFACE. Sir, I beg you will do me the honour to sit down — I entreat you, sir.

SIR OLIVER. Dear sir — there's no occasion. — [*Aside.*] Too civil by half!

---

l.30 speculative benevolence: *benevolence that never amounts to anything practical.*
l.47 complaisance: *self-satisfied air.*

JOSEPH SURFACE. I have not the pleasure of knowing you, Mr. Stanley; but I am extremely happy to see you look so well. You were nearly related to my mother, I think, Mr. Stanley?

60 SIR OLIVER. I was, sir; so nearly that my present poverty, I fear, may do discredit to her wealthy children, else I should not have presumed to trouble you.

JOSEPH SURFACE. Dear sir, there needs no apology; — he that is in distress, though a stranger, has a right to claim kindred with the wealthy. I am sure I wish I was one of that class, and had it in my power to offer you even a small relief.

SIR OLIVER. If your uncle, Sir Oliver, were here, I should have a friend.

70 JOSEPH SURFACE. I wish he was, sir, with all my heart: you should not want an advocate with him, believe me, sir.

SIR OLIVER. I should not need one — my distresses would recommend me. But I imagined his bounty would enable you to become the agent of his charity.

JOSEPH SURFACE. My dear sir, you were strangely misinformed. Sir Oliver is a worthy man, a very worthy man; but avarice, Mr. Stanley, is the vice of age. I will tell you, my good sir, in confidence, what he has done for me has been a mere nothing; though people, I know, have thought
80 otherwise, and for my part, I never chose to contradict the report.

SIR OLIVER. What! has he never transmitted you bullion — rupees — pagodas?

---

ll.73-4 his bounty ... charity: *what he has done for you would enable you to do something for me on his behalf.*
1.82 bullion: *gold or silver in bars, before being turned into coin.*
1.83 rupee: *an Indian coin;* pagodas (*probably so called because of a pagoda or deity stamped on it*): *another Indian silver coin*

JOSEPH SURFACE. Oh, dear sir, nothing of the kind! No, no; a few presents now and then — china, shawls, congo tea, avadavats, and Indian crackers — little more, believe me.

SIR OLIVER. [*Aside*]. Here's gratitude for twelve thousand pounds! — Avadavats and Indian crackers!

JOSEPH SURFACE. Then, my dear sir, you have heard, I doubt not, of the extravagance of my brother: there are 90 very few would credit what I have done for that unfortunate young man.

SIR OLIVER. [*Aside*]. Not I, for one!

JOSEPH SURFACE. The sums I have lent him! Indeed I have been exceedingly to blame; it was an amiable weakness; however, I don't pretend to defend it — and now I feel it doubly culpable, since it has deprived me of the pleasure of serving you, Mr. Stanley, as my heart dictates.

SIR OLIVER. [*Aside*]. Dissembler! — [*Aloud.*] Then, sir, you can't assist me?   100

JOSEPH SURFACE. At present, it grieves me to say, I cannot; but, whenever I have the ability, you may depend upon hearing from me.

SIR OLIVER. I am extremely sorry ——

JOSEPH SURFACE. Not more than I, believe me; to pity, without the power to relieve, is still more painful than to ask and be denied.

SIR OLIVER. Kind sir, your most obedient humble servant.

JOSEPH SURFACE. You leave me deeply affected, Mr. Stanley. — [*Calls to* SERVANT.] William, be ready to open the 110 door.

SIR OLIVER. Oh, dear sir, no ceremony.

JOSEPH SURFACE. Your very obedient.

SIR OLIVER. Your most obsequious.

1.86 avadavat: *a small Indian song-bird;* crackers: *parrots.*

JOSEPH SURFACE. You may depend upon hearing from me, whenever I can be of service.

SIR OLIVER. Sweet sir, you are too good!

JOSEPH SURFACE. In the meantime I wish you health and spirits.

120 SIR OLIVER. Your ever grateful and perpetual humble servant.

JOSEPH SURFACE. Sir, yours as sincerely.

SIR OLIVER. [*Aside*]. Charles! you are my heir.   [*Exit.*

JOSEPH SURFACE. This is one bad effect of a good character; it invites application from the unfortunate, and there needs no small degree of address to gain the reputation of benevolence without incurring the expense. The silver ore of pure charity is an expensive article in the catalogue of a man's good qualities; whereas the sentimental French

130 plate I use instead of it makes just as good a show, and pays no tax.

Re-enter ROWLEY

ROWLEY. Mr. Surface, your servant: I was apprehensive of interrupting you, though my business demands immediate attention, as this note will inform you.

JOSEPH SURFACE. Always happy to see Mr. Rowley, [*Aside*]. — a rascal. — [*Reads the letter.*] Sir Oliver Surface! — My uncle arrived!

ROWLEY. He is, indeed: we have just parted — quite well, after a speedy voyage, and impatient to embrace his

140 worthy nephew.

JOSEPH SURFACE. I am astonished! — [*Calls to* SERVANT.] William! stop Mr. Stanley, if he's not gone.

ROWLEY. Oh! he's out of reach, I believe.

JOSEPH SURFACE. Why did you not let me know this when you came in together?

---

l.126 address: *skill*.
ll.129-30 French plate: *the meaning is 'imitation silver'*.

ROWLEY. I thought you had particular business. But I must be gone to inform your brother, and appoint him here to meet your uncle. He will be with you in a quarter of an hour.

JOSEPH SURFACE. So he says. Well, I am strangely over- 150 joyed at his coming. — [*Aside.*] Never, to be sure, was anything so unlucky!

ROWLEY. You will be delighted to see how well he looks.

JOSEPH SURFACE. Oh! I'm overjoyed to hear it. — [*Aside.*] Just at this time!

ROWLEY. I'll tell him how impatiently you expect him.

JOSEPH SURFACE. Do, do; pray give my best duty and affection. Indeed, I cannot express the sensations I feel at the thought of seeing him. — [*Exit* ROWLEY.] Certainly his coming just at this time is the cruellest piece of ill for- 160 tune. [*Exit.*

SCENE II. *A Room in Sir Peter Teazle's House*

Enter MRS. CANDOUR *and* MAID

MAID. Indeed, ma'am, my lady will see nobody at present.

MRS. CANDOUR. Did you tell her it was her friend Mrs. Candour?

MAID. Yes, ma'am; but she begs you will excuse her.

MRS. CANDOUR. Do go again; I shall be glad to see her, if it be only for a moment, for I am sure she must be in great distress. — [*Exit* MAID.] Dear heart, how provoking! I'm not mistress of half the circumstances! We shall have the whole affair in the newspapers, with the names of the parties at length, before I have dropped the story at a 10 dozen houses.

Enter SIR BENJAMIN BACKBITE

Oh, dear Sir Benjamin! you have heard, I suppose ——

SIR BENJAMIN. Of Lady Teazle and Mr. Surface ——

MRS. CANDOUR. And Sir Peter's discovery ——

SIR BENJAMIN. Oh, the strangest piece of business, to be sure!

MRS. CANDOUR. Well, I never was so surprised in my life. I am so sorry for all parties, indeed.

20 SIR BENJAMIN. Now, I don't pity Sir Peter at all: he was so extravagantly partial to Mr. Surface.

MRS. CANDOUR. Mr. Surface! Why, 'twas with Charles Lady Teazle was detected.

SIR BENJAMIN. No, no, I tell you: Mr. Surface is the gallant.

MRS. CANDOUR. No such thing! Charles is the man. 'Twas Mr. Surface brought Sir Peter on purpose to discover them.

SIR BENJAMIN. I tell you I had it from one ——

MRS. CANDOUR. And I have it from one ——

30 SIR BENJAMIN. Who had it from one, who had it ——

MRS. CANDOUR. From one immediately. But here comes Lady Sneerwell; perhaps she knows the whole affair.

Enter LADY SNEERWELL

LADY SNEERWELL. So, my dear Mrs. Candour, here's a sad affair of our friend Lady Teazle!

MRS. CANDOUR. Ay, my dear friend, who would have thought ——

LADY SNEERWELL. Well, there is no trusting appearances; though, indeed, she was always too lively for me.

MRS. CANDOUR. To be sure, her manners were a little too
40 free; but then she was so young!

LADY SNEERWELL. And had, indeed, some good qualities.

MRS. CANDOUR. So she had, indeed. But have you heard the particulars?

LADY SNEERWELL. No; but everybody says that Mr. Surface ——

SIR BENJAMIN. Ay, there; I told you Mr. Surface was the man.

MRS. CANDOUR. No, no: indeed it was Charles.

LADY SNEERWELL. Charles! You alarm me, Mrs. Candour!

MRS. CANDOUR. Yes, yes; he was the lover. Mr. Surface, to 50 do him justice, was only the informer.

SIR BENJAMIN. Well, I'll not dispute with you, Mrs. Candour; but, be it which it may, I hope that Sir Peter's wound will not ——

MRS. CANDOUR. Sir Peter's wound! Oh, mercy! I didn't hear a word of their fighting.

LADY SNEERWELL. Nor I, a syllable.

SIR BENJAMIN. No! what, no mention of the duel?

MRS. CANDOUR. Not a word.

SIR BENJAMIN. Oh, yes: they fought before they left the 60 room.

LADY SNEERWELL. Pray, let us hear.

MRS. CANDOUR. Ay, do oblige us with the duel.

SIR BENJAMIN. *Sir*, says Sir Peter, immediately after the discovery, *you are a most ungrateful fellow.*

MRS. CANDOUR. Ay, to Charles ——

SIR BENJAMIN. No, no — to Mr. Surface — *a most ungrateful fellow; and old as I am, sir*, says he, *I insist on immediate satisfaction.*

MRS. CANDOUR. Ay, that must have been to Charles; for 'tis 70 very unlikely Mr. Surface should fight in his own house.

SIR BENJAMIN. Gad's life, ma'am, not at all — *giving me immediate satisfaction.* — On this, ma'am, Lady Teazle, seeing Sir Peter in such danger, ran out of the room in strong hysterics, and Charles after her, calling out for hartshorn and water; then, madam, they began to fight with swords ——

Enter CRABTREE

1.76 hartshorn: *spirits of hartshorn; akin to sal volatile.*

CRABTREE. With pistols, nephew, pistols! I have it from undoubted authority.

80 MRS. CANDOUR. Oh, Mr. Crabtree, then it is all true!

CRABTREE. Too true, indeed, madam, and Sir Peter is dangerously wounded ——

SIR BENJAMIN. By a thrust in segoon quite through his left
side ——

CRABTREE. By a bullet lodged in the thorax.

MRS. CANDOUR. Mercy on me! Poor Sir Peter!

CRABTREE. Yes, madam; though Charles would have avoided
the matter, if he could.

MRS. CANDOUR. I told you who it was; I knew Charles was
90 the person.

SIR BENJAMIN. My uncle, I see, knows nothing of the matter.

CRABTREE. But Sir Peter taxed him with the basest ingratitude ——

SIR BENJAMIN. That I told you, you know ——

CRABTREE. Do, nephew, let me speak! — and insisted on
immediate ——

SIR BENJAMIN. Just as I said ——

CRABTREE. Odds life, nephew, allow others to know something too! A pair of pistols lay on the bureau (for Mr. Sur-
100 face, it seems, had come home the night before late from
Salthill, where he had been to see the Montem with a
friend, who has a son at Eton), so, unluckily, the pistols
were left charged.

---

l.83 in segoon: *same as 'in seconde', a fencing term for the second
position of defence.*

l.85 the thorax: *the part of the trunk between the neck and the
abdomen.*

ll.100-2 from Salthill, where he had been to see the Montem with a
friend, who has a son at Eton: *it was the custom at that time for
Eton boys every three years to proceed on Whit-Tuesday to the
mound (ad montem) called Salthill, near the Bath Road, and there
to collect from passers-by money which they called salt money after
the Roman practice of paying a 'salarium' (salary) to soldiers in the
form of salt.*

SIR BENJAMIN. I heard nothing of this.

CRABTREE. Sir Peter forced Charles to take one, and they fired, it seems, pretty nearly together. Charles's shot took effect, as I tell you, and Sir Peter's missed; but what is very extraordinary, the ball struck against a little bronze Shakespeare that stood over the fire-place, grazed out of the window at a right angle, and wounded the postman, 110 who was just coming to the door with a double letter from Northamptonshire.

SIR BENJAMIN. My uncle's account is more circumstantial, I confess; but I believe mine is the true one, for all that.

LADY SNEERWELL. [Aside]. I am more interested in this affair than they imagine, and must have better information.
[Exit.

SIR BENJAMIN. Ah! Lady Sneerwell's alarm is very easily accounted for.

CRABTREE. Yes, yes, they certainly do say — but that's neither here nor there.   120

MRS. CANDOUR. But, pray, where is Sir Peter at present?

CRABTREE. Oh! they brought him home, and he is now in the house, though the servants are ordered to deny him.

MRS. CANDOUR. I believe so, and Lady Teazle, I suppose, attending him.

CRABTREE. Yes, yes; and I saw one of the faculty enter just before me.

SIR BENJAMIN. Hey! who comes here?

CRABTREE. Oh, this is he: the physician, depend on't.

MRS. CANDOUR. Oh, certainly! it must be the physician; 130 and now we shall know.

Enter SIR OLIVER SURFACE

CRABTREE. Well, doctor, what hopes?

---

l.111 a double letter: *a letter written on two sheets, for which double postage used to be charged.*
l.126 one of the faculty: *one of the medical faculty, i.e. a doctor.*

MRS. CANDOUR. Ay, doctor, how's your patient?

SIR BENJAMIN. Now, doctor, isn't it a wound with a small-sword?

CRABTREE. A bullet lodged in the thorax, for a hundred!

SIR OLIVER. Doctor! a wound with a small-sword! and a bullet in the thorax! — Oons! are you mad, good people?

SIR BENJAMIN. Perhaps, sir, you are not a doctor?

140 SIR OLIVER. Truly, I am to thank you for my degree, if I am.

CRABTREE. Only a friend of Sir Peter's, then, I presume. But, sir, you must have heard of his accident?

SIR OLIVER. Not a word!

CRABTREE. Not of his being dangerously wounded?

SIR OLIVER. The devil he is!

SIR BENJAMIN. Run through the body ——

CRABTREE. Shot in the breast ——

SIR BENJAMIN. By one Mr. Surface ——

CRABTREE. Ay, the younger.

150 SIR OLIVER. Hey! what the plague! you seem to differ strangely in your accounts: however, you agree that Sir Peter is dangerously wounded.

SIR BENJAMIN. Oh, yes, we agree in that.

CRABTREE. Yes, yes, I believe there can be no doubt of that.

SIR OLIVER. Then, upon my word, for a person in that situation, he is the most imprudent man alive; for here he comes, walking as if nothing at all was the matter.

Enter SIR PETER TEAZLE

Odds heart, Sir Peter! you are come in good time, I promise you; for we had just given you over!

160 SIR BENJAMIN. [*Aside to* CRABTREE]. Egad, uncle, this is the most sudden recovery!

---

ll.134-5 a small-sword: *a light sword for fencing.*
l.136 for a hundred: *as we might say 'ten to one'.*

SIR OLIVER. Why, man! what do you out of bed with a small-sword through your body, and a bullet lodged in your thorax?

SIR PETER. A small-sword and a bullet!

SIR OLIVER. Ay; these gentlemen would have killed you without law or physic, and wanted to dub me a doctor, to make me an accomplice.

SIR PETER. Why, what is all this?

SIR BENJAMIN. We rejoice, Sir Peter, that the story of the 170 duel is not true, and are sincerely sorry for your other misfortune.

SIR PETER. [*Aside*]. So, so; all over the town already!

CRABTREE. Though, Sir Peter, you were certainly vastly to blame to marry at your years.

SIR PETER. Sir, what business is that of yours?

MRS. CANDOUR. Though, indeed, as Sir Peter made so good a husband, he's very much to be pitied.

SIR PETER. Plague on your pity, ma'am! I desire none of it.

SIR BENJAMIN. However, Sir Peter, you must not mind the 180 laughing and jests you will meet with on the occasion.

SIR PETER. Sir, sir! I desire to be master in my own house.

CRABTREE. 'Tis no uncommon case, that's one comfort.

SIR PETER. I insist on being left to myself: without ceremony, I insist on your leaving my house directly!

MRS. CANDOUR. Well, well, we are going, and depend on't, we'll make the best report of it we can.   [*Exit*.

SIR PETER. Leave my house!

CRABTREE. And tell how hardly you've been treated. [*Exit*.

SIR PETER. Leave my house!   190

SIR BENJAMIN. And how patiently you bear it.   [*Exit*.

SIR PETER. Fiends! vipers! furies! Oh, that their own venom would choke them!

SIR OLIVER. They are very provoking indeed, Sir Peter.

Enter ROWLEY

ROWLEY. I heard high words: what has ruffled you, sir?

SIR PETER. Pshaw! what signifies asking? Do I ever pass a day without my vexations?

ROWLEY. Well, I'm not inquisitive.

SIR OLIVER. Well, Sir Peter, I have seen both my nephews in 200 the manner we proposed.

SIR PETER. A precious couple they are!

ROWLEY. Yes, and Sir Oliver is convinced that your judgment was right, Sir Peter.

SIR OLIVER. Yes, I find Joseph is indeed the man, after all.

ROWLEY. Ay, as Sir Peter says, he is a man of sentiment.

SIR OLIVER. And acts up to the sentiments he professes.

ROWLEY. It certainly is edification to hear him talk.

SIR OLIVER. Oh, he's a model for the young men of the age! — but how's this, Sir Peter? you don't join us in your 210 friend Joseph's praise, as I expected.

SIR PETER. Sir Oliver, we live in a wicked world, and the fewer we praise the better.

ROWLEY. What! do you say so, Sir Peter, who were never mistaken in your life?

SIR PETER. Pshaw! plague on you both! I see by your sneering you have heard the whole affair. I shall go mad among you!

ROWLEY. Then, to fret you no longer, Sir Peter, we are indeed acquainted with it all. I met Lady Teazle coming 220 from Mr. Surface's so humbled, that she deigned to request me to be her advocate with you.

SIR PETER. And does Sir Oliver know all this?

SIR OLIVER. Every circumstance.

SIR PETER. What, of the closet and the screen, hey?

SIR OLIVER. Yes, yes, and the little French milliner. Oh, I have been vastly diverted with the story! ha! ha! ha!

SIR PETER. 'Twas very pleasant.

SIR OLIVER. I never laughed more in my life, I assure you: ah! ah! ah!

SIR PETER. Oh, vastly diverting! ha! ha! ha!   230

ROWLEY. To be sure, Joseph with his sentiment! ha! ha! ha!

SIR PETER. Yes, yes, his sentiments! ha! ha! ha! Hypocritical villain!

SIR OLIVER. Ay, and that rogue Charles to pull Sir Peter out of the closet: ha! ha! ha!

SIR PETER. Ha! ha! 'twas devilish entertaining, to be sure!

SIR OLIVER. Ha! ha! ha! Egad, Sir Peter, I should like to have seen your face when the screen was thrown down: ha! ha!

SIR PETER. Yes, yes, my face when the screen was thrown 240 down: ha! ha! ha! Oh, I must never show my head again!

SIR OLIVER. But come, come, it isn't fair to laugh at you neither, my old friend; though, upon my soul, I can't help it.

SIR PETER. Oh, pray don't restrain your mirth on my account: it does not hurt me at all! I laugh at the whole affair myself. Yes, yes, I think being a standing jest for all one's acquaintance a very happy situation. Oh, yes, and then of a morning to read the paragraphs about Mr. S —, Lady T —, and Sir P —, will be so entertaining!   250

ROWLEY. Without affectation, Sir Peter, you may despise the ridicule of fools. But I see Lady Teazle going towards the next room; I am sure you must desire a reconciliation as earnestly as she does.

SIR OLIVER. Perhaps my being here prevents her coming to you. Well, I'll leave honest Rowley to mediate between you; but he must bring you all presently to Mr. Surfaces, where I am now returning to expose hypocrisy.

SIR PETER. Ah, I'll be present at discovering yourself there
260 with all my heart; though 'tis a vile unlucky place for
discoveries.

ROWLEY. We'll follow. [*Exit* SIR OLIVER SURFACE.

SIR PETER. She is not coming here, you see, Rowley.

ROWLEY. No, but she has left the door of that room open,
you perceive. See, she is in tears.

SIR PETER. Certainly a little mortification appears very becoming in a wife. Don't you think it will do her good to
let her pine a little?

ROWLEY. Oh, this is ungenerous in you!

270 SIR PETER. Well, I know not what to think. You remember
the letter I found of hers evidently intended for Charles?

ROWLEY. A mere forgery, Sir Peter! laid in your way on purpose. This is one of the points which I intend Snake shall
give you conviction of.

SIR PETER. I wish I were once satisfied of that. She looks this
way. What a remarkably elegant turn of the head she has!
Rowley, I'll go to her.

ROWLEY. Certainly.

SIR PETER. Though, when it is known that we are reconciled,
280 people will laugh at me ten times more.

ROWLEY. Let them laugh, and retort their malice only by
showing them you are happy in spite of it.

SIR PETER. I' faith, so I will! and, if I'm not mistaken, we
may yet be the happiest couple in the country.

ROWLEY. Nay, Sir Peter, he who once lays aside suspicion ——

SIR PETER. Hold, Master Rowley! if you have any regard for
me, never let me hear you utter anything like a sentiment:
I have had enough of them to serve me the rest of my life.
[*Exeunt.*

---

l.266 mortification: *being thoroughly annoyed with oneself.*
l.287 sentiment: *a high moral pronouncement.*

SCENE III. *The Library in Joseph Surface's House*

Enter JOSEPH SURFACE *and* LADY SNEERWELL

LADY SNEERWELL. Impossible! Will not Sir Peter immediately be reconciled to Charles, and of course no longer oppose his union with Maria? The thought is distraction to me.

JOSEPH SURFACE. Can passion furnish a remedy?

LADY SNEERWELL. No, nor cunning either. Oh, I was a fool, an idiot, to league with such a blunderer!

JOSEPH SURFACE. Sure, Lady Sneerwell, I am the greatest sufferer; yet you see I bear the accident with calmness.

LADY SNEERWELL. Because the disappointment doesn't reach 10 your heart; your interest only attached you to Maria. Had you felt for her what I have for that ungrateful Charles, neither your temper nor hypocrisy could prevent your showing the sharpness of your vexation.

JOSEPH SURFACE. But why should your reproaches fall on me for this disappointment?

LADY SNEERWELL. Are you not the cause of it? Had you not a sufficient field for your roguery in imposing upon Sir Peter, and supplanting your brother, but you must endeavour to wrong his wife? I hate such an avarice of 20 crimes; 'tis an unfair monopoly, and never prospers.

JOSEPH SURFACE. Well, I admit I have been to blame. I confess I deviated from the direct road of wrong, but I don't think we're so totally defeated neither.

LADY SNEERWELL. No!

JOSEPH SURFACE. You tell me you have made a trial of Snake since we met, and that you still believe him faithful to us?

LADY SNEERWELL. I do believe so.

JOSEPH SURFACE. And that he has undertaken, should it be 30 necessary, to swear and prove, that Charles is at this time contracted by vows and honour to your ladyship, which some of his former letters to you will serve to support?

LADY SNEERWELL. This, indeed, might have assisted.

JOSEPH SURFACE. Come, come; it is not too late yet. — [*Knocking at the door.*] But hark! this is probably my uncle, Sir Oliver: retire to that room; we'll consult farther when he is gone.

LADY SNEERWELL. Well, but if he should find you out too?

40 JOSEPH SURFACE. Oh, I have no fear of that. Sir Peter will hold his tongue for his own credit's sake — and you may depend on it I shall soon discover Sir Oliver's weak side!

LADY SNEERWELL. I have no diffidence of your abilities: only be constant to one roguery at a time.

JOSEPH SURFACE. I will, I will! — [*Exit* LADY SNEERWELL.] So! 'tis confounded hard, after such bad fortune, to be baited by one's confederate in evil. Well, at all events, my character is so much better than Charles's, that I certainly — hey! — what — this is not Sir Oliver, but old 50 Stanley again. Plague on't that he should return to tease me just now! I shall have Sir Oliver come and find him here — and ——

Enter SIR OLIVER SURFACE

Gad's life, Mr. Stanley, why have you come back to plague me at this time? You must not stay now, upon my word.

SIR OLIVER. Sir, I hear your uncle Oliver is expected here, and though he has been so penurious to you, I'll try what he'll do for me.

JOSEPH SURFACE. Sir, 'tis impossible for you to stay now, so 60 I must beg —— Come any other time, and I promise you, you shall be assisted.

SIR OLIVER. No: Sir Oliver and I must be acquainted.

JOSEPH SURFACE. Zounds, sir! then I insist on your quitting the room directly.

SIR OLIVER. Nay, sir ——

---

l.43 diffidence of your abilities: *i.e. every confidence in your abilities.*

JOSEPH SURFACE. Sir, I insist on't! — Here, William! show this gentleman out. Since you compel me, sir, not one moment — this is such insolence.   [*Going to push him out.*

Enter CHARLES SURFACE

CHARLES SURFACE. Heyday! what's the matter now? What the devil, have you got hold of my little broker here? 70 Zounds, brother, don't hurt little Premium. What's the matter, my little fellow?

JOSEPH SURFACE. So! he has been with you too, has he?

CHARLES SURFACE. To be sure, he has. Why, he's as honest a little —— But sure, Joseph, you have not been borrowing money too, have you?

JOSEPH SURFACE. Borrowing! no! But, brother, you know we expect Sir Oliver here every ——

CHARLES SURFACE. O Gad, that's true! Noll mustn't find the little broker here, to be sure.   80

JOSEPH SURFACE. Yet Mr. Stanley insists ——

CHARLES SURFACE. Stanley! why, his name's Premium.

JOSEPH SURFACE. No, sir, Stanley.

CHARLES SURFACE. No, no, Premium.

JOSEPH SURFACE. Well, no matter which — but ——

CHARLES SURFACE. Ay, ay, Stanley or Premium, 'tis the same thing, as you say; for I suppose he goes by half a hundred names, besides A. B. at the coffee-house.

[*Knocking.*

JOSEPH SURFACE. 'Sdeath! here's Sir Oliver at the door. — Now I beg, Mr. Stanley ——   90

CHARLES SURFACE. Ay, ay, and I beg, Mr. Premium ——

SIR OLIVER. Gentlemen ——

JOSEPH SURFACE. Sir, by Heaven you shall go.

---

ll.87-8 goes by half a hundred names, besides A. B. at the coffee-house: *appointments were often made at coffee-houses without the names of the parties being disclosed.*

CHARLES SURFACE. Ay, out with him, certainly!

SIR OLIVER. This violence ——

JOSEPH SURFACE. Sir, 'tis your own fault.

CHARLES SURFACE. Out with him, to be sure.

[Both forcing SIR OLIVER *out.*

Enter SIR PETER *and* LADY TEAZLE, MARIA, *and* ROWLEY

SIR PETER. My old friend, Sir Oliver — hey! What in the name of wonder — here are dutiful nephews — assault
100   their uncle at a first visit!

LADY TEAZLE. Indeed, Sir Oliver, 'twas well we came in to rescue you.

ROWLEY. Truly it was; for I perceive, Sir Oliver, the character of old Stanley was no protection to you.

SIR OLIVER. Nor of Premium either: the necessities of the former could not extort a shilling from that benevolent gentleman; and with the other I stood a chance of faring worse than my ancestors, and being knocked down without being bid for.

110 JOSEPH SURFACE. Charles!

CHARLES SURFACE. Joseph!

JOSEPH SURFACE. 'Tis now complete!

CHARLES SURFACE. Very.

SIR OLIVER. Sir Peter, my friend, and Rowley too — look on that elder nephew of mine. You know what he has already received from my bounty; and you also know how gladly I would have regarded half my fortune as held in trust for him: judge then my disappointment in discovering him to be destitute of truth, charity, and gratitude!

120 SIR PETER. Sir Oliver, I should be more surprised at this declaration, if I had not myself found him to be mean, treacherous, and hypocritical.

LADY TEAZLE. And if the gentleman pleads not guilty to these, pray let him call me to his character.

SIR PETER. Then, I believe, we need add no more: if he knows himself, he will consider it as the most perfect punishment, that he is known to the world.

CHARLES SURFACE. [*Aside*]. If they talk this way to Honesty, what will they say to me, by and by?

[SIR PETER, LADY TEAZLE, *and* MARIA *retire*

SIR OLIVER. As for that prodigal, his brother, there —— 130

CHARLES SURFACE. [*Aside*]. Ay, now comes my turn: the family pictures will ruin me!

JOSEPH SURFACE. Sir Oliver — uncle, will you honour me with a hearing?

CHARLES SURFACE. [*Aside*]. Now, if Joseph would make one of his long speeches, I might recollect myself a little.

SIR OLIVER [*to* JOSEPH SURFACE]. I suppose you would undertake to justify yourself?

JOSEPH SURFACE. I trust I could.

SIR OLIVER [*to* CHARLES SURFACE]. Well, sir! — and you 140 could justify yourself too, I suppose?

CHARLES SURFACE. Not that I know of, Sir Oliver.

SIR OLIVER. What! — Little Premium has been let too much into the secret, I suppose?

CHARLES SURFACE. True, sir; but they were family secrets, and should not be mentioned again, you know.

ROWLEY. Come, Sir Oliver, I know you cannot speak of Charles's follies with anger.

SIR OLIVER. Odds heart, no more I can; nor with gravity either. Sir Peter, do you know the rogue bargained with 150 me for all his ancestors; sold me judges and generals by the foot, and maiden aunts as cheap as broken china.

CHARLES SURFACE. To be sure, Sir Oliver, I did make a little free with the family canvas, that's the truth on't. My ancestors may rise in judgment against me, there's no denying it; but believe me sincere when I tell you — and upon

my soul I would not say so if I was not — that if I do not appear mortified at the exposure of my follies, it is because I feel at this moment the warmest satisfaction in seeing
160 you, my liberal benefactor.

SIR OLIVER. Charles, I believe you. Give me your hand again: the ill-looking little fellow over the settee has made your peace.

CHARLES SURFACE. Then, sir, my gratitude to the original is still increased.

LADY TEAZLE [*advancing*]. Yet, I believe, Sir Oliver, here is one whom Charles is still more anxious to be reconciled to.
[*Pointing to* MARIA.

SIR OLIVER. Oh, I have heard of his attachment there; and, with the young lady's pardon, if I construe right — that
170 blush ——

SIR PETER. Well, child, speak your sentiments!

MARIA. Sir, I have little to say, but that I shall rejoice to hear that he is happy; for me, whatever claim I had to his attention, I willingly resign to one who has a better title.

CHARLES SURFACE. How, Maria!

SIR PETER. Heyday! what's the mystery now? While he appeared an incorrigible rake, you would give your hand to no one else; and now that he is likely to reform I'll warrant you won't have him!

180 MARIA. His own heart and Lady Sneerwell know the cause.

CHARLES SURFACE. Lady Sneerwell!

JOSEPH SURFACE. Brother, it is with great concern I am obliged to speak on this point, but my regard to justice compels me, and Lady Sneerwell's injuries can no longer be concealed. [*Opens the door.*

Enter LADY SNEERWELL

SIR PETER. So! another French milliner! Egad, he has one in every room in the house, I suppose!

---

l.171 sentiments: *here 'what you feel'*.

LADY SNEERWELL. Ungrateful Charles! Well may you be surprised, and feel for the indelicate situation your perfidy has forced me into.   190

CHARLES SURFACE. Pray, uncle, is this another plot of yours? For, as I have life, I don't understand it.

JOSEPH SURFACE. I believe, sir, there is but the evidence of one person more necessary to make it extremely clear.

SIR PETER. And that person, I imagine, is Mr. Snake. — Rowley, you were perfectly right to bring him with us, and pray let him appear.

ROWLEY. Walk in, Mr. Snake.

Enter SNAKE

I thought his testimony might be wanted: however, it happens unluckily, that he comes to confront Lady Sneerwell, 200 not to support her.

LADY SNEERWELL. A villain! Treacherous to me at last! Speak, fellow, have you too conspired against me!

SNAKE. I beg your ladyship ten thousand pardons: you paid me extremely liberally for the lie in question; but I unfortunately have been offered double to speak the truth.

SIR PETER. Plot and counter-plot, egad!

LADY SNEERWELL. [*Going*]. The torments of shame and disappointment on you all!

LADY TEAZLE. Hold, Lady Sneerwell — before you go, let 210 me thank you for the trouble you and that gentleman have taken, in writing letters from me to Charles, and answering them yourself; and let me also request you to make my respects to the scandalous college, of which you are president, and inform them, that Lady Teazle, licentiate, begs leave to return the diploma they granted her, as she leaves off practice, and kills characters no longer.

LADY SNEERWELL. You too, madam! — provoking — insolent! May your husband live these fifty years!   [*Exit.*

---

l.215 licentiate: *a degree in continental universities.*

220 SIR PETER. Oons! what a fury!

LADY TEAZLE. A malicious creature, indeed!

SIR PETER. What! not for her last wish?

LADY TEAZLE. Oh, no!

SIR OLIVER. Well, sir, and what have you to say now?

JOSEPH SURFACE. Sir, I am so confounded, to find that Lady
    Sneerwell could be guilty of suborning Mr. Snake in this
    manner, to impose on us all, that I know not what to say:
    however, lest her revengeful spirit should prompt her to
    injure my brother, I had certainly better follow her
230   directly. For the man who attempts to —— [*Exit.*

SIR PETER. Moral to the last!

SIR OLIVER. Ay, and marry her, Joseph, if you can. Oil and
    vinegar! — egad you'll do very well together.

ROWLEY. I believe we have no more occasion for Mr. Snake
    at present?

SNAKE. Before I go, I beg pardon once for all, for what-
    ever uneasiness I have been the humble instrument of
    causing to the parties present.

SIR PETER. Well, well, you have made atonement by a good
240   deed at last.

SNAKE. But I must request of the company, that it shall
    never be known.

SIR PETER. Hey! what the plague! are you ashamed of having
    done a right thing once in your life?

SNAKE. Ah, sir, consider — I live by the badness of my
    character; and, if it were once known that I had been be-
    trayed into an honest action, I should lose every friend I
    have in the world.

SIR OLIVER. Well, well — we'll not traduce you by saying
250   anything in your praise, never fear. [*Exit* SNAKE.

SIR PETER. There's a precious rogue!

---

l.226 suborning: *to incite some one secretly to a wrongful action.*

LADY TEAZLE. See, Sir Oliver, there needs no persuasion now to reconcile your nephew and Maria.

SIR OLIVER. Ay, ay, that's as it should be, and, egad, we'll have the wedding to-morrow morning.

CHARLES SURFACE. Thank you, dear uncle.

SIR PETER. What, you rogue! don't you ask the girl's consent first?

CHARLES SURFACE. Oh, I have done that a long time — a minute ago — and she has looked yes.   260

MARIA. For shame, Charles! — I protest, Sir Peter, there has not been a word ——

SIR OLIVER. Well, then, the fewer the better; may your love for each other never know abatement.

SIR PETER. And may you live as happily together as Lady Teazle and I intend to do!

CHARLES SURFACE. Rowley, my old friend, I am sure you congratulate me; and I suspect that I owe you much.

SIR OLIVER. You do, indeed, Charles.

SIR PETER. Ay, honest Rowley always said you would   270 reform.

CHARLES SURFACE. Why, as to reforming, Sir Peter, I'll make no promises, and that I take to be a proof that I intend to set about it. But here shall be my monitor — my gentle guide. — Ah! can I leave the virtuous path those eyes illumine?
Though thou, dear maid, shouldst waive thy beauty's sway,
Thou still must rule, because I will obey:
An humble fugitive from Folly view,
No sanctuary near but Love and you: [*To the audience.* 280
You can, indeed, each anxious fear remove,
For even Scandal dies, if you approve.   [*Exeunt All.*